A Woman's Life

Treetops

Elizabeth Cole

Doctors and Women

Home Before Dark

The Cage

Handsome Man

Looking for Work

Susan Cheever

Note Found in a Bottle

My Life as a Drinker

SIMON & SCHUSTER

SIMON & SCHUSTER
Rockefeller Center
1230 Avenue of the Americas
New York, NY 10020

SIMON & SCHUSTER and colophon are
registered trademarks of Simon & Schuster Inc.

Designed by Ruth Lee

Manufactured in the United States of America

1   3   5   7   9   10   8   6   4   2

Library of Congress Cataloging-in-Publication Data
Cheever, Susan.
Note found in a bottle : my life as a drinker / Susan Cheever.
p.   cm.
1. Cheever, Susan.   2. Alcoholics—Biography.   I. Title.
HV5293.C49A3   1999
362.292'092—dc21
[B]   98-26463   CIP
ISBN 0-684-80432-8

For my children

Contents

CONTENTS

There is another sort of blow that comes from within—that you don't feel until it's too late to do anything about it, until you realize with finality that in some regard you will never be as good again.

—F. Scott Fitzgerald,
The Crack-Up

Note Found in a Bottle

Drinking with Daddy

*M*y grandmother Cheever taught me how to embroider, how to say the Lord's Prayer, and how to make a perfect dry martini. She showed me how to tilt the gin bottle into the tumbler with the ice, strain the iced liquid into the long-stemmed martini glass, and add the vermouth. "Just pass the bottle over the gin," she explained in the genteel Yankee voice that had made her gift shop such a success that she was able to support her sons and husband. I watched enthralled as she twisted the lemon peel with her tiny white hands and its oil spread across the shimmery surface. I was six.

New York City in the 1940s was a postwar paradise. Soldiers brought back wonderful, exotic war souvenirs: bamboo hats from the Philippines and delicate lacquered boxes from Japan. It was all sunlight and promise and hope in those days. The streets were safe; the shopkeepers knew everyone who lived on the block. The women wore dresses and high-heeled shoes, and the men all wore brimmed felt hats trimmed with grosgrain ribbon.

Outside our windows the Queensboro Bridge rumbled with traffic. The avenues around our apartment building filled up with the rounded shapes of Buicks and Chevrolets. My father bought a secondhand Dodge for trips to the country, and he parked it across Fifty-ninth Street, right next to the bridge, so that we could admire it from the windows of our apartment. It was that car, I always thought, that wrecked our golden New York City life. In that car my parents started taking us out to visit friends who had moved from the city to the suburbs. These friends were always telling my parents how great the suburbs were. In the suburbs there were wonderful public schools. In the suburbs a young family could have their own house. In the suburbs there was plenty of outdoors for children to run around in, and a community of like-minded parents. In 1951 we moved.

Every evening at six o'clock, right on schedule—because almost everything in those days was right on schedule—the grown-ups in the suburbs would prepare for what they called their preprandial libation. They twisted open the caps of the clinking, golden bottles and filled the opalescent ice bucket, brought out the silver martini shaker and the heart-shaped strainer and the frosted glasses, and the entire mood would change. I loved those mood changes even then.

I loved the paraphernalia of drinking, the slippery ice trays that I was allowed to refill and the pungent olives, which were my first childhood treat, and I loved the way the adults got loose and happy and forgot that I was just a child. I loved the way the great men would sit down so close to me that I smelled their smell of tweed and cigarette smoke and whiskey and tell me their best stories about hiding in a tree at Roosevelt's inauguration, or dodging German bullets in France, or meeting Henry James as a doddering old man in a London club; and the way the women would let me play with their lipsticks and mirrors and would show off the mysterious lacy underwear that held up their silky stockings and held in their tiny waists.

I knew that, like them, I would grow up and get married. My husband would have a job in the city, and I would iron his Brooks shirts; I would learn to cook pork chops in cream sauce and to bake a Lady Baltimore cake, and I would serve cheese and crackers and nuts at parties and take care of my children. We would have a little house, just like my parents', and on vacations we would take our children to visit them just as they took us to visit Bamie in Quincy and Binney and Gram in New Haven and New Hampshire. In the evenings, I would greet my homecoming hubby with the ice bucket and the martini shaker. On Sunday mornings we would have Bloody Marys. In the summer we would stay cool with gin and tonics. In the winter we would drink Manhattans. In good times we would break out champagne, in bad times we would dull the pain with stingers. I was already well acquainted with the miraculous medicinal powers of alcohol. My mother dispensed two fingers of whiskey for stomach pain and beer for other digestive problems. Gin was an all-purpose anesthetic.

Drinking was part of our heritage, I understood. My earliest memories were of my father playing backgammon with my grandmother over a pitcher of martinis. The Cheevers had come over in 1630 on the *Arbella,* the flagship of the Winthrop fleet. The trash came over on the *Mayflower,* my father always said. The best Puritans, the Puritans like us waited until it was clear that the New World was a place worthy of our attention. I learned that the *Arbella* set sail with three times as much beer as water, along with ten thousand gallons of wine. Hemingway had called rum "liquid alchemy." Jack London and John Berryman and Dylan Thomas had written about the wonders of drinking. Brendan Behan came to visit and, with a drink in his hand, sang to me. "The bells of hell go ting-a-ling-a-ling for you but not for me," he sang. "O death where is thy sting-a-ling-a-ling, O grave thy victory?"

I found out about divorce at around the same time that I learned that the Russians, who lived on the other side of the world, had enough atomic power to blow us all up. These two ways in which my life could be shattered by outside forces wielded by irrational adults seemed equally terrifying. From what I saw around me in those idyllic suburbs, marriage was not a happy state. Often when there were parties at our house, the merriment of the first cocktails became sparring and loud arguing before the dessert was served.

By the time we had lived in the suburbs a few years, my father's suburban stories were appearing regularly in *The New Yorker*. Although we couldn't afford to join a country club, or buy a new car—all our cars were secondhand—as a family we had a status conferred on us by my father's success. My father liked to tell divorce stories: he loved the story of how Gert Simon had left her husband while he was at work in his office in New York City—taking the children, the furniture, and even the pets and leaving nothing at all—so that he came back at nightfall to an empty house where he thought his home was.

Divorce was still pretty rare though. If you ask me, the grown-ups were too dressed up for the indignities of divorce court. They still had their hats on every time they went out.

When they got clinically depressed, when their adulteries caught up with them, when all the martinis in the world weren't enough to blot out the pain of their humanness, they killed themselves quietly. No one talked about it. They hanged themselves with their hats on.

Thunderbird off the Coast of Maine

*I*n 1951 we had moved to Scarborough, New York, to a small house on Beechwood, the estate of Frank Vanderlip, a man who had been president of the National City Bank and had been a mover and shaker in the administrations of Presidents Herbert Hoover and Warren Harding. The Vanderlips had five children, and houses had been built for them on the estate near the white-columned mansion. A guest house, Little Beech, with its own squash court had been built next to the big house. The house we moved into, Beech Twig, or more jocularly, Beech Nuts, had been a toolshed before it was remodeled and rented out.

In one way Beech Nuts was a terrific find, a new start for our young family. In another way it was a nightmare. Every now and then one of the Vanderlips would show up on our doorstep with a friend from her own class, a woman in a Dior shirtwaist, named Janie or Edie, to see if the friend might like the house as a country pied-à-terre. "It would be divine having you here!" the Vanderlip would croon to the friend.

My father would serve drinks and play host to the ladies who were talking about renting our home. After they left there would be angry silence. I could almost feel the fear in the air. My mother would go upstairs in tears. My father would pour a drink and brood. "I don't know where we'll go," he would say. "I don't know where we'll go." Then, when Janie or Edie decided *not* to rent Beech Nuts, we felt both relieved and rejected. Our own house wasn't grand enough for some rich woman's weekend place. We hadn't behaved well. Somehow the Janies and Edies of this world had taken our measure and found us wanting.

In my memory it rained for three years: gray rain, slanting past the windows of the dark little house in the corner of the wall and soaking the earth of my mother's flower gardens, rain swamping the velvety lawns and drowning the roots of the great beech and willow trees around the Big House, rain on the roof of the school bus, and rain outside the windows of the school, making the playing fields muddy and slippery.

Our suburban neighborhood with its picture-book exteriors often seemed to breed brutality. We turned on each other too; we were as scary to each other as we were to outsiders. As a girl I expected to be caught, stripped of my clothes, fondled and mocked and sent home crying—if I was dumb enough to be surprised alone by the older boys. I took a different way home from school every day. When my own band caught a younger kid, we filled their pockets with worms or gravel. We got a kick out of watching them cry for mercy. Sometimes we made them cut themselves and bleed for our benefit. They rarely told their parents.

When we weren't hurting the younger kids we were spying on the older ones. On hot summer nights we girls patrolled the streets of the suburbs, looking for couples we could scare with hoots and snickers. We snuck out of our houses at night to peer through the windows at the adult parties on Linden Circle and Sleepy Hollow Road. We watched through the picture windows as our parents' friends had cocktails in their living rooms and got lecherous in their kitchens and bedrooms. We watched from behind a tree as one of the Palumbo cousins kissed one of the Scarborough School teachers and slid his hand under the hem of her circle skirt.

The railroad tracks ran between the town of Scarborough and the Hudson River, and for all of us the tracks with their deadly, electrified third rail were one giant, fascinating dare. Sometimes we put pennies on the tracks. Sometimes we sat and watched the trains—looking like rich kids' toys—as they came around the curve from Tarrytown and Philipse Manor. Usually we just taunted each other as the train approached, daring our friends to get closer and closer to the rails. The point was to get as near as we could to the deafening noise, the whoosh of air, and the presence of death as the train passed. In that moment the world was blotted out, and then there was the great relief and the sharp joy of being alive.

The summer I turned twelve, we rented a house on the coast of Maine owned by my parents' friends, the Spears. We took a slim, teen-age Irish girl from another part of Scarborough along as my baby-sitter. In the land of lobster I declined to eat lobster. My parents lived by classical music; my father played Chopin on the piano. I listened to the soupy music that was the languorous prelude to rock and roll. In the meantime, my baby-sitter took up with a lobsterman named Mike Watkins and proceeded to drive him wild. She would tell my parents we were going for a walk, and we would take off in Mike's brown Ford. They necked and drank beer in the front, while I sat in the back with the car light on and read the fan magazines my parents wouldn't buy me. Trying to block out the noises of their courtship, the cooing and the rustling, which was often punctuated by a sudden gasp or the snap of a strap, I read about the sex lives of the Hollywood stars. There were lots of stories about Anita Ekberg.

Sometimes they left me alone in the car while they went for a walk along the rocky shore and disappeared for a while. In the glove compartment, Mike had a flat bottle, which they took with them. I sat in the backseat, ignoring the roar of the surf roiling against the rocks nearby, and read by the dim light of the bulb on the Ford's ceiling how Joe DiMaggio had been spotted at some starlet's house while Marilyn was off on the set of *The Seven Year Itch*.

Mike was poor. He lived with his big, scrawny coast-of-Maine family. The successful men in his world were lobster fishermen, up before dawn, on creaky, leaky boats in icy water, to trap balky crustaceans, which were bought on the dock by the crooked middlemen up from Boston. The failures were just drunks, watching TV while sitting on broken-down couches in the living room of anyone who would have them, anyone who would buy them a beer. By my family's standards, the baby-sitter was poor. She lived in a small house next to the Post Road, and her father didn't even read *The New Yorker* or even *The New York Times*. But to Mike Watkins she was a princess.

Still, as the summer passed, I could almost feel the depression lift off our family's shoulders. My father had finished his novel, and we were going to Italy. My mother was pregnant. We were going somewhere, not like the other suburban families, trapped forever in the limbo of six o'clock cocktails, meaningless conversations, pathetic lechery, and Sunday-morning hangovers so bad that starting the car felt like shooting off a howitzer.

The Weight of Air

*M*y first whole drink was a few swallows of homemade grappa from a thick green goblet. I stood in the circle of adults who had gathered to wish our family well on the eve of our trip to Italy in 1956 the autumn after we got back from Maine. There was Sam the gardener, with his wrinkled brown face and overalls, and Angelo Palumbo and his wife, with her gray bun and her shapeless black dress, and the other Italians who worked on the estate where we lived. I winced as the raw grappa hit my throat. The grown-ups' faces were all red. Everyone was laughing. No one smelled of tweed, or the Chesterfields my mother smoked or the Camels my father smoked. The air in the apartment above the estate's garage was filled with a sweet, nauseating smell. On the stove pots filled with eggplant and tomato sauce simmered in the heat.

"It was Sunday afternoon and from her bedroom Amy could hear the Beardens coming in, followed a little while later by the Farquarsons and the Parminters. She went on reading *Black Beauty* until she felt in her bones that they might be eating something good," my father wrote at the time before we went to Italy. The story, "The Sorrows of Gin," like most of his short stories, is about drinking. My father wrote fiction, but in the seething air of our household, an air rich with imagined events and invented characters, it was often hard to tell what was real and what was a story. "Fiction is not crypto-autobiography" my father was fond of saying; true, but our lives often seemed fictional—my mother sometimes acted as if my father had invented her, and she resented it. My brother Ben once said that, in that household, he always felt like a minor character in someone else's novel. Even now, as I reread "The Sorrows of Gin," it seems to me that the fictional Amy is as good a portrait of me at that age as anything I can recall. The story continues:

Then she closed her book and went down the stairs. The living room door was shut, but through it she could hear the noises of loud talk and laughter. They must have been gossiping or worse because they all stopped talking when she entered the room.

"Hi, Amy," Mr. Farquarson said.

"Mr. Farquarson spoke to you, Amy," her father said.

"Hello, Mr. Farquarson," she said. By standing outside the group for a minute, until they had resumed their conversation, and then by slipping past Mrs. Farquarson, she was able to swoop down on the nut dish and take a handful.

"Amy!" Mr. Lawton said.

"I'm sorry, Daddy," she said, retreating out of the circle towards the piano.

"Put those nuts back," he said.

"I've handled them, Daddy," she said.

"Well, pass the nuts, dear," her mother said sweetly. "Perhaps someone else would like nuts."

Amy filled her mouth with the nuts she had taken, returned to the coffee table, and passed the nut dish.

"Thank you, Amy," they said, taking a peanut or two.

"How do you like your new school, Amy?" Mr. Bearden asked.

"I like it," Amy said. "I like private schools better than public schools. It isn't so much like a factory."

"What grade are you in?" Mrs. Bearden asked.

"Fourth," she said.

Her father took Mr. Parminter's glass and his own, and got up to go into the dining room and refill them. She fell into the chair he had left vacant.

"Don't sit in your father's chair, Amy," her mother said, not realizing that Amy's legs were worn out from riding a bicycle while her father had done nothing but sit around all day.

As she walked towards the French doors, she heard her mother beginning to talk about the new cook. It was a good example of the interesting things they found to talk about.

"You better put your bicycle in the garage," her father said, returning with the fresh drinks, "it looks like rain."

Amy went out on the terrace and looked at the sky, but it was not very cloudy, it wouldn't rain, and his advice like all the advice he gave her was superfluous. They were always at her. "Put your bicycle away." "Open the door for Grandmother, Amy." "Feed the cat." "Do your homework." "Pass the nuts." "Help Mrs. Bearden with her parcels." "Amy, please try and take more pains with your appearance."

Our year in Italy passed in the splendid combination of exhilaration and disappointment that characterized all our family adventures. We had a great time; nothing changed. Soon enough we were back in the limiting confines of Beech Nuts. It wasn't that I had a miserable childhood—I didn't—it was that I was a miserable child. The most effective distraction from the misery was also the most painful problem—my asthma. Some of my father's family had asthma, and of course my parents both chain-smoked, but whether it was nature or nurture, by the time I was nine or ten it became clear that my bronchi were particularly vulnerable to constriction.

My first memories of the asthma involved being taken into the delicious rose light of my parents' bedroom and allowed between the silky white of their sheets. Then there were drugs, needles, which miraculously allowed me to breathe. I loved those needles, the rush of oxygen, the sudden ease of breathing, that thing which everyone else did without thinking. Breathing began to obsess me as early as I can remember. Every time I had to go somewhere important, I wondered if the asthma would come. It often began slowly, with signs that were discernible only to me. Breathing in, I would feel a slight catch in my throat.

Air, usually light and invisible, would begin to take on a weight of its own. I would clear it with a cough, but I knew what was happening; only I knew, and the knowledge took hold of my throat like a strangler. Heavier every second, the air I needed to stay conscious would soon be like a precious substance that had to be drawn into my lungs with sucking force. Within a half hour I would be bent over double, struggling for breath, my lungs making terrifying wheezing, shrieking sounds while everyone wondered what was happening to me. "What on earth?" they said.

Later in my life I got better at hiding the attacks. I set up a rhythm of coughing to disguise the wheezing, sucking sounds. I found a way of leaning forward so that my desperate straining for air wasn't quite so obvious. I found that coffee and later a generous shot of whiskey were ways to delay the strangling contractions. Once they began, I found that gin relaxed my bronchial spasms. The doctors gave me pills that lessened the asthma and made my heart beat so fast that I had to lie down.

Sometimes, even after I felt it starting, I could relax myself and go into someone's bathroom and calm the attack down. Bathrooms were always the easiest places to breathe. Sometimes I got away with it. But the asthma itself was less terrifying than the fear that it might double me over at any minute, during a test at school, during a tennis lesson at the Sconset Casino in Nantucket; when some fancy friends of my parents came for Sunday lunch, when a guy finally noticed me enough to ask if I'd like to come watch a soccer game on the field below the school.

The attacks were unreliable in that they could arrive at any time—but they were also reliable. Sunday night, staring at the wall, thinking about school the next day, I could suddenly feel that the air going into my lungs had substance. I could feel the dust motes, the bits of pollen beginning to irritate my bronchial tubes, which I imagined as tunnels of sensitivity taking air from my mouth to my lungs. Sure enough, by midnight I'd be wheezing and gasping, my fever elevated from the struggle, my shoulders hunched forward as my mother brought me Benadryl and started up the vaporizer and called the doctor.

Thirty years after the worst of my attacks, I read a biography of Theodore Roosevelt in which his asthma, which also often began Sunday night and became crippling by Monday morning, was described in detail. No one knows what this is like except another asthmatic. It came as a shock to me that a man of great distinction also suffered from a condition that seemed to me like a personal mark of shame. I was the only kid I knew who had asthma, the only kid who went through the terror of the beginning of an attack, the gasping hunger for breath at the middle, and the skinned, embryonic feeling of re-birth at the end.

My asthma was triggered by all sorts of substances and events, but animals and Mondays were almost certain to have me struggling. I prayed for hives, hay fever, any other allergic symptom instead of this dreadful, embarrassing, frightening thing. My prayers went unanswered. I read Somerset Maugham's *Of Human Bondage,* and I knew how Philip felt when he confidently prayed to have his clubfoot removed and was as surprised as he was disappointed in the morning. My asthma was a badge of difference, something I took with me everywhere, invisible but powerful.

First Love

*I*n the spring of my sophomore year at college, I brought my First Love, a fellow student, home for a visit. My father hated him on sight. He immediately forbade any physical contact between us in his house. We were not to kiss or hold hands indoors. "No necking in the parlor!" he shouted, and he meant it. At lunch my father poured us both martinis from the silver shaker. My First Love slept most of the afternoon and woke up with a headache.

By September my First Love and I were sleeping together. He rented an apartment off campus in an Italian neighborhood at the bottom of College Hill. We shared the bathroom with four other apartments. We lived on red wine and hamburger that he bought for a dollar a pound. I soon learned, again without knowing I had learned it, that I could keep my father's disapproval at bay by restricting my sexual activity to the sons of his friends and, later, to the friends of his friends.

After a Christmas Eve party that year, another man drove me home and kissed me. He had a deep voice and a reassuring, plummy accent. They had kicked him out of Groton for insubordination and drinking, but he had already learned to elongate his *a*'s and rattle his *r*'s. His name was Palmer; he was the son of my father's best friend. I was dazzled by his sexy condescension, his handsome grin, his worn-out tweeds, his pink Brooks Brothers shirts and the way he moaned "Oh Susie, Oh Susie," using my childhood name. By that time, everyone else called me Susan.

The first week-end I spent with Palmer, it was raining. He was writing a novel about a cabdriver. He never ate meals. His house, a red clapboard saltbox built into the side of a hill, was under construction. He had torn out one wall and planned to build an addition. The rain came in through the holes. In the mornings we hacked away with rusty shovels at what was supposed to be the new foundation; in the afternoon we drew plans and drank. Neighbors dropped by to talk, and sometimes the evening turned into a party. We drew plans for bay windows and plans for grand flights of stairs and told stories about the grander parties we would have when the addition was finished. I spent a lot of weekends with Palmer. I never slept with him, but for a long time I thought I was in love with him. I was sad when he fell in love with other women, and when he married Kathy and then Wendy and then Cindy.

And all that time, all that time that I was growing up, drinking seemed as much a part of life, as ordinary a part of life, as eating or even breathing. No one in our family saw what was happening. No one talked about it. My father drank; my mother cooked. At home we laughed while alcohol twined it-self around us like a choking, deadly, invisible vine. There were plenty of early signs. Guests were always falling down the stairs; above the level of the banister, there were scuff marks on the wall from flying feet. People who came for lunch fre-quently had to be put to bed during the course of the after-noon. Sometimes they stayed for days. The family cars made lots of trips to the body shop. In the evenings there were terri-ble fights. Almost any disagreement quickly escalated into a deadly silence or an apocalyptic rage.

Of course everyone around me was drinking, and when they drank, I drank too. Of course I had heard about alcoholics: they were old men in trench coats who had lost everything, or they were housewives who nipped at the sherry and were passed out on the kitchen floor when their children needed to be picked up from school. It never would have occurred to me or anyone around me that there was any connection, any con-nection at all, between the problems I had—at school, with men—and the way I drank.

I remember the moment I discovered what the fuss was all about. My First Love and I were apart and quarreling. I was alone, sitting in my parents' dining room on the ground floor of the beautiful house in Ossining to which my family had re-cently moved. Everything should have been wonderful, but I felt skinned and lonely. I was filled with a sharp longing—for my First Love, I thought. I knew he didn't love me. He could never love me enough. I felt a tearing sensation, a yearning that was almost physical.

Then my father walked toward me with a gin and tonic. It was a hot, hot afternoon. I took a sip. The drink was fizzy and tasted of sugar and quinine and then, almost as an aftertaste, the steely gin. I took a swallow, gulping down the sweetness to savor the metallic taste of the gin.

I began to feel better. The yearning lessened. Outside, the lawns were steaming in the heat, the delphiniums and zinnias drooped on their stems. I could feel myself relaxing, as if I had suddenly become part of the great scheme of things. I could almost feel the earth turning in the rich summer air. There would be many men in my life, I knew. I was young, beautiful, smart. Dust motes in the bright air began to look like stars. My father turned on the record player, and the buoyant strains of Handel filled the room. The barges were moving down the Thames, the sun glinting off the instruments in the horn section. I was swept away in the feelings of the music and the heat and the cool glass under my fingers and the taste of gin. I was swept away from my pain, from those sharp, terrible feelings; I was swept away for many years.

We Are Always True to Brown

The coolest people at Brown didn't go there at all, they went to the Rhode Island School of Design down the hill on Benefit Street. RISD had a wonderful small museum, and RISD students had all kinds of freedom, and the girls had long hair and short, hot affairs, and the men never wore the dorky jackets and ties favored by Brown men for Big Occasions. The men had names like Lars and Bolte—Brown men were all called Mike and Joe—and the women's names all ended in h: Dinah, Sarah, Susannah. My friend Pam's friend Sybil went there, and Pam and I would go down to RISD and just drink it in: the freedom, the sex, the way Sybil's friend Jane Hall was writhing on the floor one night—because she was so horny, she said—and the way she was begging a guy named David Whitney to do it to her.

"Do it to me," she moaned, as she twisted her body toward him. "Come on, David, do it to me."

It was twilight, and no one had bothered to turn on the

lights. Jane's sinuous body snaked and swerved around the impassive David. David and Jane had both gone to the Woodstock Country School—I had gone to Woodstock too, a year or so later—so they took me on faith and let me stand and watch their little drama. I was fascinated.

David said no; Jane writhed. She twisted her long hair around her breasts; her shirt fell open, and we could see that her nipples were hard. David turned away, acting bored. Jane stretched her body to its full length, grabbed onto his ankles, and pulled herself toward his feet. He shook her free. "Get Lars to fuck you," he said. Back up in the dormitory lounge, my classmates were sitting around in bobby sox with their hair in rollers, comparing charm tips from *Seventeen* magazine.

Now I'm proud to have gone to Brown, but at the time, all that mattered to me was that I didn't get into Harvard. During my early months with my First Love, I was also seeing an older student named Ken. Ken was handsome and smart and rich; naturally I preferred the elusiveness of my First Love. One evening, when I had agreed to meet Ken at my dormitory and attend a lecture with him, I dallied too long with my First Love. I arrived at the dorm to find a note from Ken. "Cheever," it said, "you blew it!" In a moment my feelings were electrified. I saw in a flash that I had lost the only man I had ever really cared about. How could I have been so stupid? What appeal did my pallid First Love have next to the amazing Ken? I took a long walk to assuage my pain. It was too late now. You blew it, Ken had written. I had blown it. I felt the loss viscerally, as if I had been punched. What a fool I was.

When I returned to the dorm I was thrilled to find Ken waiting for me, smiling eagerly. He had saved a seat for me at the lecture because he had hoped I would come. Did I want to have dinner? Did I want to take a walk? For the second time in an hour my feelings reversed themselves. What kind of square would save a seat for a woman he had just broken up with? What kind of sucker would come back for more of the same? I told Ken to go away and secretly congratulated myself on remaining true to my First Love.

My First Love and I settled into a comfortable routine. After dinner we met and studied, and necked on the grass if it was warm enough. Sometimes we went to the new Brown library across from Memorial Hall and the ornate Robinson Building. The more I saw of him, the more I became aware of how much he smoked pot and how hard that made it for him to function in the very regulated world of the university. He missed a meeting with the dean of students. Sometimes he slept through classes. Sometimes he had to take a day off and go up to Boston to "see his friends" on Symphony Road. He came back from these trips with plastic bags filled with marijuana. In the spring he was asked to take a semester off.

That summer, to keep me away from him, my father got me a job on the clip desk at *Time* magazine. I sat at the clip desk, reading all the newspapers, clipping almost every article and filing it for the magazine's morgue. There was lots of sex at *Time* in those days, sex between the editors (all men) who often had to work late in their glamorous jobs, and the researchers and clip desk girls (all girls) who worked right along with them. Every editor had a big office with his own personal researcher stationed in an anteroom space. Every editor had a wife and children comfortably stashed in a nice house in Westchester, or Montclair, or Darien. Every editor was required to work late nights, and hotel rooms were provided for those so dedicated that they sometimes never even got home to sleep. It was a formula for adultery, and it worked very well. Some of us called it two-*Time* magazine.

We went to homecoming weekend that fall. Brown lost as it always did, but we were in love. At one of the homecoming parties, we all drank a lot. I looked over at my First Love, flirting with a classmate, and decided that we should get engaged. We had a huge fight the next day, the upshot of which was that he agreed that we were engaged. In my head we were already married with children and struggling to start—my dream, of course—our own alternative school like the one I had gone to in some place like Woodstock, Vermont.

My First Love's family lived on a leafy residential street in a brown shingle house on the corner. Behind it in a huge white frame house with French windows and porches and trailing vines lived his grandmother, his father's mother. His father had gone to Brown. Everyone said he was smart. In the evenings after dinner he sat down with the daily crossword. There was always a glass of whiskey at his elbow. He did the crossword in ink, he was so good at it. One night I decided to sit down and help him with the crosswords. As I worked out the spaces for down and across I slowly realized, with horror, that he paid no attention to the clues in the crossword, he just filled it in with any words that would fit. I didn't know what to say.

"My mother says you're very demanding," my First Love said to me when things started falling apart.

We lived in fear of war in those days. Some contractor had built a model bomb shelter in downtown Providence, and we had picketed it in protest against everything it stood for. Inside, there were shelves of canned foods and a machine that looked like a huge meat grinder, which cranked in fresh air, and four rudimentary bunk beds. It was as dark as a bad dream in there, and a couple of the demonstrators used the narrow bunks to demonstrate the victory of eros over agape.

And a few weeks later, listening to the car radio, I had a sense that the world had started spinning faster. President Kennedy had been shot; President Kennedy was dead. I was wearing a maroon sweater, and my First Love drove us up from his apartment to the campus in a jaw-clenched silence. It was over this that we had our second big fight. He wanted to watch everything on television. There was only one place for him that long weekend in November: with the group of students in front of the television in the College Union, the Blue Room lounge. I didn't want to join him. I thought the world was coming to an end. I didn't want to die watching television. I joined a group that was drinking beer in a nearby apartment.

To say that my comfortable illusion of normalcy through coupledom never survived the weekend of the assassination is to commit the pathetic fallacy with history—to imagine that we are somehow at the center of the universe so that our lives run a parallel course to world events. After that weekend, though, it was never the same.

SIX

Graduation

I was twenty; it was 1964. We were all reading Hemingway and wearing Capezio flats and blouses with Peter Pan collars. We were all going to join the Peace Corps. We were all going to get married. All my life I had known who I was by identifying myself as for or against some institution or person, and my identity as my First Love's fiancée was the ultimate identification. Now, as the first man who had ever wanted me drifted away, it was as if my soul was being wrenched right out of my body. I knew I would never be as close to anyone else ever again.

That summer I moved into a run-down shingle house on Linnaen Street in Cambridge with five other girls who were going to Harvard. In the long, lonely evenings, I bicycled around Cambridge, dreaming of a love that would make me whole again. Every time I drove out to my First Love's family's house in the suburbs, I turned onto Storrow Drive hoping that my First Love would be as glad to see me as he once had been; hoping that I wouldn't cling to him, that I wouldn't reveal in a cadence or a remark how abandoned I felt. The time I spent in his family's house—where we had once been so happy that the whole place seemed to glow from within—was intensely painful. I knew what to do about it. I asked my First Love's father to make me a drink, and he obliged with pleasure.

Back in Cambridge, I met another man in my Irish Poetry class, and I rode to Walden Pond on the back of his motorcycle. We drank white wine out of huge gallon jugs. My new boyfriend thought I was wonderful; he thought my First Love was crazy to let me go. Once, after we sat on the banks of the Charles and watched the hot summer evening fade, he said that he thought he was falling in love with me. Later, when I looked down toward the river from the window of his room in Eliot House, I remember I wondered who was going to pick up our beer cans.

By the time I headed south with another man and a bottle of gin, I was cut loose, as if I had just been waiting for my First Love to dump me so that I could shed the boring chrysalis of being someone's girlfriend and become my real, free self. Courtland Cleves and I drove down to Miami, flew to Nassau, and took the primitive mail boat through the Bahamas to Inagua to visit Lee. Lee was my best friend at college—actually she was one of my many best friends. Courtland was in love with her, and I too was half in love with her, her silences, her grace, her elusive intelligence. Lee was a girl my father would have adored, I thought. But on the way through South Carolina on a rainy afternoon, I lay my head in Courtland's lap as he drove. I felt so sleepy. Within a few hours we were hungrily touching each other in a cheap hotel in Savannah, telling each other that we couldn't, we couldn't because it would be so disloyal to Lee.

The Bahamas were sparklingly beautiful and untouched in those days. As the mail boat docked on each island, children, women with baskets on their heads, and the village goats came out to greet us. There were endless white beaches fringed with palms, the water was transparent aqua, we watched from our seat in the stern of the boat as great cumulus clouds formed and re-formed in the bright blue sky. One night we ended up in my bunk with him on top of me; he put the bottle of gin on the floor.

Back at school, I had to see my First Love with his new girlfriend all the time. Everyone said she looked like me. I went out with whoever asked me. I went out with Jay, who had his own apartment. Before dinner he showed me how to drink boilermakers—a jigger of whiskey and a can of beer. We drank boilermakers and listened to his favorite music, which happened to be Sibelius. Then we drove to an Italian restaurant. Then we went back to his place and drank more boilermakers and listened to more Sibelius. I don't remember much of what happened after that. He drove me home, and his car ran out of gas a few blocks from my dormitory. I remember going out the next morning to see if his car was still there where it had stalled at the curb on Waterman Street.

In my senior year I thought I had a weight problem, so I stopped eating. When I was hungry, I would eat three cookies from a stash that I kept in a bag in my dorm. Sometimes I fasted for days; I liked the light-headed feeling fasting gave me, and I liked getting thin. Then I would break the fast. I spent hours thinking about what I might eat. Usually it was something odd but delicious, like a jar of strawberry jam or a can of salted peanuts. Then I would get sick and vomit. Food was a problem, but drinking was the answer to a series of problems. I don't even remember what I drank most of the time. I just drank the way everyone I knew drank. Sometimes I forgot what happened when I drank; so did everyone. Sometimes I felt sick the next day; big deal, that's what I thought.

In the spring of 1965, when I got to his house the night of our graduation dance at Brown, my old friend Larry was sitting on the roof. Larry had gone to Brown, but after he graduated he moved to Cambridge. He wasn't expecting me. I had fled Providence and the graduation dance. No one asked me to the dance. The man I thought I was in love with had asked my best friend. I was on an orange juice diet. Larry seemed glad to see me. He opened a bottle of wine. When he found out it was graduation weekend, he even thought maybe we should drive back down to Providence and go to the dance. So I had a date after all. But by that time we were on our second or third bottle, sweating it out on the roof. I didn't know what Larry wanted or what he thought. I only knew that he had provided me with a scrap of safety, and I clung to it. I didn't intend to sleep with him. I didn't intend to sleep with anyone I wasn't engaged to, or about to be engaged to. That night, when we went to bed, he pulled the covers back, and I saw that the sheets were stained with blood. I pretended not to notice. I was afraid to ask where it came from, but it frightened me, and I kept my clothes on.

About a year ago I ran into Larry in Mill Valley, California. I was giving a reading in a restaurant, and he came loping up afterwards. We talked for a few minutes. He told me that he had realized he had a drinking problem. He explained that he had joined Alcoholics Anonymous. The other people at the reading buzzed around us, waiting for autographs. Then he explained that he had decided that he didn't need AA. He talked about being an architect and how everyone in architecture was so uptight that he had decided to start his own firm in Oakland. Then he walked away across the Mill Valley Plaza. I still didn't ask him about the blood.

Rocky Mountain Buzz

*E*very Sunday morning my father went to the Boyers' for a ritual drink. Martinis were mixed in a Boyer family silver shaker and poured into hefty glasses. The smell of gin and the way the martinis caught against the sides of the glass are as much part of my memory as the jollity and generosity that seemed to take over the gathering while shakerful after shakerful was consumed. We children ate the olives out of the drinks and out of the jar, played with the dogs, and sank into the Boyers' deep, cushioned furniture.

One winter Sunday morning, my red convertible stalled, flooded, and then went dead. My mother had taken the other car to do some grocery shopping, or go to some civic meeting, or do something else that we deemed of no importance. We were stranded. There was no way to get to the Boyers'. My father called the local Volkswagen place, and they sent a cab to fetch us. I had a shiny new green convertible in time to take everyone to the Boyers' without missing a drink.

I drove the green car to my first job after college, a job as an English teacher in Carbondale, Colorado, in a school that shared the alternative-education philosophies of my beloved Woodstock Country School. I had never had a job. I had never been west of Pennsylvania. I drove across the great prairies under the limitless sky and slept in Iowa City and North Platte and watched the snow-capped Rockies materialize from the plains like a great stage set.

In the afternoons, after English class, I would drive the car up into the mountains above Marble or above Glenwood Springs until I ran out of road. I drove uphill on the asphalt and then on gravel and then on narrow dirt tracks above the timberline, above where the aspens made golden streaks in the stands of pines, and the air was clear and scarce and sweet. I listened to a rock station in Oklahoma City and dreamed of the prairies while I drove into the mountains. Other times I drove up to Aspen and skied all day, hanging out with the ski bums and drinking huge pitchers of beer. I rented a rancher's house above the school and parked my car behind the woodshed.

After dinner in the cafeteria we teachers would go back to our dorm rooms to read and correct papers. I always went to Ned's. Ned was another teacher who had just graduated from college—Harvard in his case—and was teaching at the Colorado Rocky Mountain School as a kind of adventure before he settled down to real life.

When we were teaching together, I spent hours in his room after dinner, reading and talking because I wasn't ready to drive home. We did our work and complained a little and congratulated ourselves a little and drank Southern Comfort. Every Wednesday night we had a pizza together at the local bar—Frank and Edie's—and drove to Glenwood Springs to the movies. We saw a lot of early Elvis movies; many of them seemed to have plots that revolved around long bus trips. Coming home together in the car, we sometimes talked about our families. From that far remove, driving up the Roaring Fork Valley toward the glistening cone of Mount Sopris, his family, the Cabots, and my family, the Cheevers, seemed quite alike.

Sometimes Ned and I would take groups of kids on overnight hiking or spelunking trips. The school's philosophy was that teachers who shared adventures with their students would be better teachers. The hiking trips called for special provisions—to our supply of Southern Comfort we added an emergency supply of Hennessy. Brandy kept us warm up there in the mountains on those freezing nights. Back in the valley, as we corrected papers, we would mix up a pitcher of orange blossoms. The recipe: one bottle of Gilbey's and a can of frozen orange juice. We sipped and corrected papers, and most of the students did very well.

By the time I turned out of the school driveway and headed home to my house on the ranch there was often so much snow that I had to follow someone else's tire tracks to find my way. Then there was a sharp left, and a two-plank bridge across the Crystal River. I would make the left and aim for the planks, threading the car between the narrow railings on either side of the bridge. Then there was a curve, and then my house, but by the time I took the sharp right around the woodshed, I had sometimes begun to miscalculate. There would be a ripping, wrenching sound, and in the morning I could see that another part of the car's fender had been torn off, or another section of the door pushed in. That was all right with me. In the spring I took the car to the repair place in Denver and flew home to New York. I rented a car for the summer; my father paid for it. In September, when I flew back to Denver, my Colorado car was as good as new.

Drinking and the
Romantic Imagination

Sometimes I hoped that Ned and I would become more than friends—I even remember rolling the sound of Mrs. Edward Cabot on my tongue after one particularly romantic interlude. We shared wonderful moments together in the sparkling air of that beautiful landscape. We were explorers together in the world of jobs after college. But most of the time I was happy to have him as a good friend and a reliable colleague. For me it was that simple.

For my father, however, it was much more complicated. Once he discovered that I was friends with Ned Cabot, that I was, perhaps, "seeing" Ned Cabot, his imagination was off to the races. This was, after all, what he had always wanted for me, or more truly, what he had always wanted for himself. Every time we talked, he asked about Ned. How was Ned? How was Ned's family? In my father's journals—which I didn't read until after his death twenty years later—he waxed poetic on the possibility of my engagement to Ned Cabot.

He imagined the way his friends might respond. He imagined, in detail, the interview that old Mr. Cabot might command at the Somerset Club or the Chilt in Boston. Mr. Cabot would ask my father if I had been brought up correctly. Was I schooled in the things that would prepare a woman to be a bride of the Cabots? Did I know how to give a dinner? How to conduct myself at a tea party? In his journals my father imagined that he would be able to assure Mr. Cabot that I knew the forks and that I had been educated in the ways of the upper classes.

At Christmas during the first year we taught together, Ned and I flew to New York, landing at night at Newark Airport. Ned was on his way home to Boston, and I had invited him to spend the night at my parents' house in Ossining. On the telephone, I could almost hear my father's excitement; this was during the years when he was drinking all the time. No one imagined that he was an alcoholic, of course. In fact he had recently savored some particularly delightful success when Frank and Eleanor Perry made a movie of his story "The Swimmer," in which my father had a cameo role. Even better, Alan Pakula had paid some handsome option money for the rights to my father's novel *The Wapshot Chronicle*. My father had taken the money and bought himself a red Karmann Ghia convertible, a two-seater with a tiny space for baggage in the back under the rear window.

Naturally it was in this car that he came to pick us up at the airport. When he met us at the gate, my father was not exactly drunk, he was just extremely exuberant; his was an exuberance, however, that had clearly been fueled with some extra gin while he waited for our flight to land. He shook Ned's hand buoyantly and led us to the curb where the little car was illegally parked.

We piled into the car with Ned curled in a fetal position in the back. My father's driving was erratic, and suffered when he frequently turned around to make a point. He smelled of gin, and in the confined space of the overheated car the smell was so thick it was almost tactile. By the time we were on the George Washington Bridge, approaching the city, Ned remembered that he had promised to stay with his cousin Nick Danforth on Riverside Drive. My father urged him to reconsider, but Ned, or what was left of him, was adamant. A prior obligation could not be changed. My father finally concurred, behaving, I'm sure he thought, in a way that Ned would recognize as the mark of a gentleman. We dropped him off at the corner of Eighty-sixth Street; a light snow began to fall.

This incident was so unremarkable that I didn't even think about it at the time. My father was often as drunk as he had been that night, and often as silly. But when I read his journals, I understood how he had done, that night, what alcoholics so often do. He had wanted something so much that he had to somehow keep it from happening; the very things that he dreamed about seemed to elude him when they were tantalizing him with their closeness.

Alabama 1965;
Mississippi 1966

I got to the Montgomery airport in the summer of 1965, and that summer and the summer after it—the summer after my first year of teaching English in Colorado—I went further and further into the heart of darkness that was the black South in the 1960s.

The lawns at Brown were velvety swaths punctuated by great maples and oaks. At Tuskegee the land around the dorms was hard-packed earth with some sparse grass. There were stray dogs everywhere, foraging, scavenging, breeding under the dorms and belonging to no one. Our group of volunteers often ate together in the Tuskegee cafeteria: meals of beans, grits, and cornbread washed down with Coke. Sometimes we got in the leader's big white car with a couple of six-packs and took field trips to swim in the lake at Auburn.

One day the leader decided that we should all go and see Selma, Alabama, and walk across the bridge where Martin Luther King had led the famous march just a few months before. Then we would have lunch in the café where the Reverend Reeb had eaten his last meal; he had been beaten to death on the sidewalk as he left. A civil rights field trip, that's what our leader called it. Locked behind the windows in the huge air-conditioned car, we glided through the streets where history had been made by our comrades.

The civil rights movement is now a part of history, but at the time it was a bunch of us kids from Ivy League colleges, driven by a sense of justice and a desire to be hip, taking a kind of magical mystery tour of the third world. Down there we went to parties and drank a lot just the way we did on our own campuses. Down there we got involved with guys and they tried to sleep with us and we tried not to let them, just like we did at home. Down there we drank Schlitz Black Label; back home we drank Bud.

In Tuskeegee I went everywhere with a skinny kid named Sammy Young and his partner, Winky Parish. One Sunday we decided to integrate the local churches. Black and White together we approached the doors of the Congregational church on Main Street, but of course they wouldn't let us in. Winky and I snuck around the back and took our places in a seated circle that turned out to be a Bible class. We sat there as each member of the class read a few verses and glared at us.

Another time we decided to integrate the Tuskeegee town meetings, which were held once a month at the town hall, an antebellum building on the central green. As the meeting of white men started, we filed into the back of the room. They glared, they twitched, they turned red. One of them, a gas station owner named Bob Segrest who was on the town council, started staring right at Sammy as if he could will him out of the room. We stayed, and afterwards we laughed together at the way they had tried to get us to leave. Later that winter, when I was very far away in Colorado, Sammy pulled up to Bob Segrest's gas station and they got into an argument and Bob Segrest shot him dead.

I was teaching English to private-school kids in the next valley over from Aspen and skiing Buckhorn and Silver Bells and the other trails on Ajax on my days off. On Saturday nights, when we mixed up our orange blossoms, we sometimes read *Time* magazine, the only national news we saw all week. That's where I read about what had happened in Tuskeegee; that's how I found out that Sammy was dead. I didn't tell anyone that I had known Sammy; it all seemed so far away. I knew what my Colorado friends would say: they would say I didn't belong in Alabama anyway.

Privately I decided to go back to the South again the next summer. My presence there had helped cause a tragedy, but that wasn't the way I saw it; the way I saw it was that I wasn't going to let them get away with killing my friend. I was under the impression that I took up a lot of space in the world, and that my actions made a huge difference to other people—except, of course, on days when I felt invisible. Any injustice drew me like a magnet. This was a painful way to live, and people who live this way often need to find ways to mitigate the pain of their experience and feelings.

I left for Mississippi in June of 1966 in summer traveling clothes: a blue-and-green Peck & Peck sleeveless linen dress and sling-back shoes from Delman, accessorized with gold shrimp earrings from Kenneth Jay Lane, and a Mark Cross suitcase packed with more of the same. No one met me in Jackson. All I had was an address on Farish Street. As I limped down the dusty street in high heels and costume jewelry, carrying my big monogrammed suitcase, everyone turned and stared. At the headquarters, up a dingy staircase on the second floor, I hid behind a door and changed into the carefully matched shorts outfit and the flats I had brought.

At first I lived in Jackson with some other civil rights workers. We slept with different families on the pleasant tree-lined streets of the black neighborhoods. In the mornings we went to meetings where nothing happened. We sat in a circle and got lectures on civil rights history. In the afternoons we hung out at Charlie's Kitchen on Farish Street, a dark restaurant which was the real headquarters of everything that was happening in Mississippi in 1966. We drank a lot of beer. We couldn't know that what was happening was a retreat, a rout. For the time being the segregationists had won, and the few of us who were still trying to register voters and form food co-ops and organize meetings—there were less than a hundred of us in Mississippi that summer as it turned out—were the last of the troops of a phantom Northern Army that had marched off beaten from the same battlefield where we took our stand.

After we had been there for about a week, we were split up. My friend Nick went down to Sunflower County—I didn't see him again for years. Another worker, Jim, went to Neshoba County. The storefront where he was working was bombed the day after he got there, and he went home to his wife. I was assigned to a man named Jake Higgins. In his rickety pickup truck, we were going to Shubuta, a small town near Meridian, in the southern part of the state. The people in Meridian needed to be registered to vote.

The first night we spent in a safe house near Philadelphia. As we drove through Neshoba County, a sheriff's car pulled off the shoulder and followed us. Jake signaled me to lie down in the back of the truck so that a white woman wouldn't be seen being ferried across the state by a black man. The sheriff—Jake said it was Sheriff Lawrence Rainey, the man who was later tried and acquitted on federal conspiracy charges arising from the killing of Andrew Goodman and his friends (their bodies hadn't been found yet)—followed us for a while and then turned left off the road. At the safe house, a man came out and hid our truck around the side of the house on a patch of red dirt. We hadn't eaten all day. I ate a package of crackers I had saved in my pocket and fell asleep on a creaky bed.

In the morning, Jake and I drove along a maze of dusty back roads until we got to the house of Shubuta's local minister, where I was going to live. It was a white frame house on a patch of grass, with no indoor plumbing; a bed had been set up in the living room for me. There was no one home. Jake explained that I would be spending my days working with him and the other SNCC volunteers.

This was the first I knew that I was working for SNCC. The Student Non-Violent Coordinating Committee was one of the most militant groups working in civil rights. By the time I was in Mississippi, they had become both uncoordinated and violent—there never seemed to be any students among the membership—and many of the SNCC leaders were calling for a ban on white people in the organization. The SNCC headquarters in Shubuta was a cramped room behind a small grocery store. The people who ran the store were an elderly couple who had been persuaded to help the cause by letting SNCC use their back room. There I met my fellow volunteers, Henry, a gentle black man from California, and John T., a scrawny white kid from Texas. Across a dusty courtyard was the rest of Jake's family. He went home for meals, and his mother frequently came over to our office to tell him to get on home and do his chores.

Jake's little kingdom was furnished with a bookshelf with dusty copies of Winston Churchill's *Diaries* and a few other history books, a pay telephone, the three of us, and two rifles. We all drank beer against the heat and plotted and planned and cleaned and recleaned the rifles. Sometimes when Jake felt we were insubordinate, he would point one of the rifles at one of us and give orders. As the afternoon heat faded, we got in the truck. Jake would drop me at a corner somewhere well off the main road. My job was to knock on doors and get people to come to a meeting we were holding at the end of the week. Mostly, people didn't answer their doors.

I would walk across the front yards with their red dirt and scrubby grass and go up on the creaky porch and look through the screen door and knock. I had bought a few simple linen shifts at Lord & Taylor that seemed perfect for Mississippi, but they were soon covered with the ubiquitous dust, and my arms were quickly sunburned. Through the screen I could see the dark shapes of whoever was in the house moving in the shadows. After I had knocked three times, I gave up.

Sometimes a scrawny dog threatened me, but I hushed it and went on about my business. I wasn't afraid of dogs; I had grown up with dogs. "Quiet!" I would say, or "Down!" in the authoritative voice I had learned for the purpose of training Labrador retrievers to sit and fetch. These dogs were different.

One afternoon a big white-and-brown mutt followed me, and as I reached the road he sank his yellow teeth into my leg. I didn't mention this to anyone.

Once or twice an old man or woman would come to the door and shoo me away. I would begin trying to tell them why I was there. I would mention the meeting. It made no difference. I was like a creature from another planet. What did a rich white girl from Westchester in her bright pink or green Capezio flats have to say to someone who was scratching out a living in the backwoods of southern Mississippi?

After a few hours of this, Jake would come looking for me in the pickup, and we'd all go back to the squalid, steamy room we called headquarters. At headquarters I often curled up in one of the deep bookcases and fell asleep. Jake amused himself during the afternoons by calling white girls who lived in the wealthy part of town. Afterwards he would talk to us about his fantasies of how he was going to go out with them and what he was going to do with them once he had them in his truck.

He looked up their names in the phone book, targeting the fanciest addresses he could find. He put on a white, preppy accent—he was a talented mimic— and pretended he was a guy who was visiting from Jackson and wanted to ask them out.

Sometimes he would put me on the phone, and I would pretend to be his sister from New York. He usually had to point the gun at me to get me to do this. Talking to these white girls, these Southern belles, I wanted to cry out for help. They were the enemy, Jake said, but as time went on *he* seemed more and more like the enemy. I knew those girls in their pink-and-white bedrooms with their stuffed animals and their flowered stationery and their prom dresses, and I wondered what I was doing there in that horrible room, in dirty clothes, drinking the beer Jake stole from his mother's refrigerator. Sometimes when I woke up in the living room of the minister's white house I longed to be at home in Westchester.

One day we went to a local segregated restaurant and tried to get served a hamburger. We sat in a circle around a wooden table and elaborately scrutinized the menu. The ceiling fan above the tables creaked and thumped, and we could smell other people's hamburgers frying on the big grill at the back of the room. No one would wait on us. The young man who was the waiter for our table was shaking with fear. Everyone in the restaurant looked terrified by our presence. Henry suggested we should leave. Jake, who knew people in the restaurant, kept yelling at them to come on over, but their faces were gray, and they turned away from him. I wondered if that was what I had come for, to scare the shit out of the people of the state of Mississippi.

That night, Jake and John T. got hold of two bottles of whiskey. After we had finished both, they went around to the front of the building and painted a target on the big glass windows of the grocery store with white paint. "Let them come and get us!" they crowed. But the two old people who ran the store felt differently. They didn't say anything to Jake, but I watched as they cautiously came out with buckets and sponges and removed the bull's-eye painted on their store. I saw two old people swabbing and scraping in the fading light of a hot Southern evening. Jake watched them as he drank a beer and jeered at them for being afraid.

Jake persuaded me that I could do better work for the cause if I bought a car. It was too much trouble driving me back to the house every night, he said. It was too much trouble having to find me on the back roads to pick me up. I called my parents, and they wired money to a bank in Meridian. The four of us, John T., Jake, Henry, and I drove into town and bought a yellow Ford Fairlane. Henry and I drove it back to Shubuta. We talked about our families, and I saw that becoming Henry's friend was the only way I would survive. I flirted with him. When he parked the car I kissed him. I sat on his lap. "What a woman like you needs is a real man," he whispered to me, and I smiled at him. "Does it bother you that I'm rich?" I asked. After that Jake didn't threaten me anymore.

Fear

One morning I woke up and decided to go home. I told the minister I was living with and he looked me straight in the eye. "I think that's a good idea," he said. I walked a mile across a scraggly green field and down a dusty road to get to a house with a telephone—I knew I couldn't call on the SNCC phone. On an ancient rotary phone in someone's front parlor, I dialed my parents, praying that they would be there. They were. Later they said I sounded very frightened. Then I called the airline and made a reservation for a flight that night from Jackson to Atlanta. When Jake drove in to pick me up for the day's work, I was already packed.

Jake was not about to let me get away with the new car. He wanted to come to Jackson with me. I said no. Henry wanted to come too, and he promised to bring the car back to Jake. I said all right, and before I knew it I had set off across Mississippi in a flashy yellow car with no license plates—the dealer

had given us a temporary paper plate that sat in the rear window—with Henry in the passenger seat. Jake had given Henry
the address of a SNCC safe house in Jackson where he could
stay. I was running scared, that was my excuse. I don't know
what Henry was thinking. He had a gentle wife at home who
wrote him nice letters.

We hadn't even gotten to Meridian when we passed a Mississippi State Trooper car at the side of the road. As I watched
in my rearview mirror, the car pulled out after us and turned
on its siren. We pulled over, and two troopers got out of their
car with guns drawn. Passing cars honked their approval as the
troopers flattened Henry up against the side of our car. I produced my New York driver's license. "I am just trying to get
back to New York where I belong," I told the troopers. They
didn't touch me but they roughed up Henry before they let us
get back in the car.

This happened three times between Meridian and Jackson:
the troopers' car pulled us over, Henry was held down against
the car while people passing by cheered the troopers on. Each
time, I verbally disowned Henry and any activities I may have
engaged in that might have displeased the law in Mississippi.
Finally, each time, they let us go. One of the cars followed us
for ten tense miles, clearly as they decided whether or not to
pull us over again and take more drastic action. "I'm sorry,
Henry," I would say after we had been driving again for a
while.

"That's okay, girl, that's okay," he would say in response.

I missed the plane. We had left Shubuta at about 10 A.M.,
and it was past dark when we pulled into the Jackson airport.
Henry had decided he didn't want me to go. Instead of hating
me, as he should have, he had decided he was in love with me.

I made a reservation on a midnight plane to Atlanta, and we repaired to Charlie's Kitchen. After a few beers, Henry persuaded me that we should go to the safe house so I could take a shower and we could rest properly. I was still shaken, and we were both covered with the red Mississippi dust kicked up from the shoulders of the roads where we had spent so much of the day.

The safe house was on a corner a few blocks down Farish Street from Charlie's. The key was in a flowerpot as Jake had promised. There was no one there. I lay down with Henry to try and sleep, and before I knew it we were kissing, kissing with all the intensity of people who had just been through hell. Then he was on top of me. I broke away for a minute. A man was standing on the sidewalk looking up at the lights of the house. I lay back down. "I'll be gentle," Henry said, his huge body pressing against mine. "I'll be gentle." I rolled away again. The white man was still standing there. "I think we're being watched," I said. Henry got up, and after he looked out, the man left. I announced my intention to get washed up; it was about 10 P.M.

I locked myself in the tiny bathroom at the back of the house and drew a bath. Henry sat against the bathroom door and chatted with me as I soaped up, rinsed off, and shaved my legs—it felt wonderful to be in a bathtub with a drain and hot and cold running water after weeks of the hose and the outhouse. But as I put my razor away, I slipped and it sliced through the flesh of my index finger, causing a geyser of blood to spurt across the bathroom.

"What is it?" Henry had heard my frightened intake of breath. "Nothing," I said, quietly, deliberately looking around for something to stanch the blood, which was now pooling on the floor. If I let him in to help, I knew what would happen. "Is that guy still out there?" I said. As Henry got up to look, I used the cover of the noise he made to slip out of the tub and reach for some old, stained towels on a shelf over the toilet. Slowly, trying to be so quiet he wouldn't know I was moving, I wrapped a towel around my finger and held it up; finally the bleeding slowed. "He's gone," Henry said, "you're taking long enough." The towel was soaked with blood. I took my extra cotton underpants out of my suitcase and bound them tightly around my finger. In the meantime I one-handedly combed out my hair and slithered into a dress and shoes.

Gradually the bleeding began to stop. Finally I was dressed. I stuffed the bloody underpants back in the shelf with the towel and used a handkerchief to wrap my finger. I turned out the bathroom light as I emerged and handed Henry my suitcase so that his hands would be busy. "You look great," he said, "I like to see my woman dressed up."

"I cut my finger," I said holding up the bunched-up handkerchief. "I guess I'll have to let you drive."

He grinned. I smiled back. I held my breath as we headed for the airport; I couldn't wait to get away from him. Now that he was driving this flashy car, Henry's mood changed. He forgot that he was in love with me and remembered his SNCC mission—to bring back the car. He didn't want to risk leaving it in the parking lot now that he was in the driver's seat. He dropped me off at the curb.

I was still afraid he was following me, so I ducked into the airport bar and ordered a martini. Still, I was afraid that Henry would somehow appear in the door to the bar. What if he decided to come to New York?

All the way down the jet way to the plane I kept looking

back as if he might be following me. In Atlanta I had to wait for a morning plane to New York. I spent the night on a molded plastic chair in the Atlanta airport. It was too uncomfortable for me to sleep, and I had a headache. My mouth felt filled with cotton. I drank airport coffee and thought back over the past weeks. I was already savoring the drama, refining the recent events of my life into a story. All my stories were dramatic, and they always featured a heroine in peril.

Note Found in a Bottle

*I*got in to Kennedy Airport at about nine in the morning and
took a cab right up to 666 Madison Avenue, to Robert's office at *The Reporter* magazine. The magazine had been started
by Max Ascoli, a friend of my parents'.

Robert was the son of old friends of my parents'. Robert
was this, my parents told me as I was growing up, Robert was
that. Robert was graduating from Harvard, Robert was marrying the beautiful so-and-so. Robert and his wife and their children were at their house on Cape Cod. Robert and his wife
were getting divorced.

One spring morning before I went to Mississippi I had just
appeared in Robert's office and he took me out to lunch. We
drank a little red that he chose from a wine list. He was the
only man I knew who wore a suit. His French cuffs were fas-
tened with a pair of gleaming spiral silver cuff links. "Sandy
made them for my mother," he said casually, as if having

Alexander Calder make you a pair of cuff links was the most natural thing in the world. He had a real job with an office, and a secretary with an English accent. He ordered martinis and scotches in restaurants. He knew how to make a drink.

After I got back from Mississippi, we spent the hot nights of summer making passionate, sweaty love in his apartment in Greenwich Village. We fucked in his bed and on the couch in his living room and even on the floor. We took showers together and walked around with no clothes on. We explored each other's bodies inch by inch as if we were discovering a hidden treasure. We drank sangria at El Faro and beer at Max's Kansas City and martinis at the Harvard Club. I was a long, long way from Meridian, Mississippi. In a few weeks I was leaving for Colorado. I felt grown-up for the first time in my life.

I was driving into New York from Ossining to have dinner with Robert every night. He lived in a second-floor apartment on Waverly Place, across from Washington Square. Occasionally, late at night, other women would call. There was a Sally and an Anne. They didn't worry me. About a week before I was leaving, he announced he was going out with a girl named Robin. I shrugged my shoulders, smiled sweetly at him, and drove home. My father was drinking gin and tonic that morning, and I joined him. I called a man I had met in Colorado and arranged to go to Rhode Island with him for the weekend. By the time I came back, just in time to leave for Colorado again, Robert had had his disastrous date with Robin and he was giving me those looks I had come to crave as surely as if they were a drug, those looks I had first gotten from my long-ago First Love.

I drove back to Carbondale and the Colorado Rocky Mountain School with Ned in his Mustang. We took turns driving and only slept once, by the side of the road in Kansas. By the time we got to Carbondale there was a mournful letter from Robert. I answered with a sprightly phone call—I was too busy to write. During the day, I taught school with the perfect backdrop of Mount Sopris twinkling down through the plate-glass windows of the classrooms. At night we mixed up our pitchers of gin and concentrated orange juice. Sometimes while we drank it started to snow.

Sometime in November, Robert called and asked me to come home for good. Although this was what I had been waiting for, I was surprised. I spent a weekend talking about it. Ned thought it was an absurd idea. But then a friend of mine who was the algebra teacher at the school suggested that Robert might not wait for me. If I wasn't around he might stray. I thought about Sally and her desperate phone calls. I imagined Robert, a tall man in a good suit, striding into Gino's with another, prettier woman—Robin perhaps. I called him and told him I was coming home.

Robert and I always started our evenings together with a drink—and we both agreed this was when the day really began. A scotch, which he mixed, and then a bottle of wine with the dinner I had cooked. Sometimes I drank some wine during the day. When we went out to dinner parties, Robert had a habit of nodding off while we were still at the table. I told him to just go and lie down if he felt sleepy. It never dawned on me that there was anything strange about this; Robert used to say that he had a touch of narcolepsy. When the "narcolepsy" hit, always in the evening, Robert would stumble from the table and lie down in the nearest place where he could stretch out—sometimes on the floor. Dinner parties with Robert's friends often rotated around his inert form.

The wedding date was set for May 6th. My mother and I went to Bendel's and ordered the dress. Robert and I went for counseling to the Reverend Michael Allen—a hip minister who had once been a magazine editor—at St. Mark's in the Bowery, a beautiful and completely inconvenient church. My father hired a fancy caterer to create a reception for three hundred in the graveyard of the church. The whole thing cost a fortune, or at least that's what my father told everyone.

My parents were more than an hour late for our prenuptial dinner. One of the ushers had ordered May wine while we waited. "What is this?" my father demanded. He always hated sweet wine, as if a taste for sweet things would compromise his masculinity. The next morning I gathered with my friends and my mother in the apartment I shared with Robert. We began to drink champagne as I got dressed. My father came to get me in the limousine; the driver got lost on the way to the church. Packed into the back of the car, dressed and veiled for my wedding, I listened as my father argued with the driver.

By the time I walked down the aisle I had drunk too much champagne to remember much. The reception reverberated with the loud congratulations of my parents' friends and the crying of Robert's two clinging children. I had my problems with these two children already. While I wanted them to love me, I certainly didn't love them. I alternately refused to see them and wanted to create a family with them at its center. Robert's psychiatrist, Dr. Iago Galdston, an elderly, infinitely distinguished White Russian who lived and practiced in his frame house in Brooklyn Heights, had given me the ultimatum a month before the wedding. In marrying Robert I was marrying his children, Dr. Galdston said. Okay, I said.

The great Dr. Galdston was the third party in my marriage to Robert. When I got back to New York, we went to see him together, and pretty soon I was seeing him alone, once a week, and Robert was occasionally being called in to be scolded for his bad behavior toward me. Dr. Galdston was my ultimate ally, my secret weapon. Robert often didn't understand me; Dr. Galdston always did. It turned out that my grandfather had known Dr. Galdston, back in the days when he was Isador Abraham Goldstone, a name he changed to Iago Galdston.

In the fall of 1967, Robert and I moved to the suburbs. Zinny Schoales, Mrs. Vanderlip's daughter, asked if we would be interested in renting Beechwood, the ninety-room mansion on the ridge, which had been unoccupied and empty since Mrs. Vanderlip died. We said we would. For three hundred dollars a month—the same price my family had once paid for the mansion's outbuilding, Beech Nuts—we leased the mansion.

We tried to keep up with the house. We gave weekend parties and drank too much. Sometimes we had terrible fights. When Robert hurt me, I drove to Brooklyn to see Dr. Galdston. He understood. I spilled out my unhappiness in the room at the back of his house that he used as a study. It was decorated like Freud's study, with kilim rugs draped over a couch and a photo of Freud on the wall. Dr. Galdston always locked the door to the study when I was there. When I left, he stood up with me and held me in his arms as if to comfort me. He knew how unhappy I was. Then he sometimes kissed me on the lips, gently pushing his tongue into my mouth. Sometimes he put a hand against my dress and cupped my breast above where my young heart lay in terrible confusion. I could hear the sounds of his wife moving around upstairs or outside in their garden. When I finally told Robert about what was happening in Dr. Galdston's office, he didn't seem alarmed. "Maybe he doesn't know that it bothers you," he said.

Bow Wow

*B*eechwood had been built in phases, beginning with a small colonial mansion and ending with the huge ballroom tacked on by Welles Bosworth at the north end of the house. It had been decorated in more recent phases, according to the taste of the moment. Robert and I slept in a room in the central part of the house, behind a columned portico. To keep us company, we bought a dog, a golden retriever we named Maisie after the Maisie in Henry James.

At one end of Beechwood there was the book-lined ballroom, with its huge fireplace, two Steinway grand pianos back to back, and a vast expanse of parquet floor. Next door there was an Italianate music room, and on the other side of the ornate dining room, a French room crowded with ormolu and gilt Empire furniture, crystal, and taffeta drapes. At the bottom of the grand staircase was the Italian section, with stucco walls, heavy beams, oil paintings in gilded frames, and a conservatory with a splashing Italian marble fountain. Above this, on the second floor, was the Chinese wing, where mandarins on silk screens gazed out over black and red lacquer furniture and screens painted with Oriental landscapes. At the center of the house was an English country nursery with dimity curtains, a mural of children frolicking, and a fireplace with THE BEECHES SAY, DEAR CHILD OBEY, carved in the marble. Next door was the nanny's chapel with a mahogany prie-dieu.

The center of the house was essentially English, with romantic oil paintings, hunting prints, William Morris wallpaper, and heavy marble fireplaces. As she grew, Maisie became the perfect accompaniment to my days of leisure as the mistress of Beechwood. She played in front of the house, and in the afternoon she gamboled around when I strolled down the velvety lawn to the formal gardens to gather flowers for the arrangement I put on the dining room table, where I served Robert dinner. She raced along beside me in the evenings when I met Robert on the way up from the railroad station. We had heard that Mr. Vanderlip's butler always met him on the path from the station with a sloe gin fizz. Maisie and I preferred to carry a pitcher of gin and tonic, or as autumn set in, a pitcher of chilled martinis.

Summer ended, and Angelo Palumbo the caretaker drained the swimming pool. In the vegetable gardens, tomatoes drooped from their vines. The smell of apples filled the Hudson Valley air. The leaves turned on the estate's great maples and beeches. Robert and I began to have terrible fights. On the way back from driving him to the station in the morning I often found myself heading for my parents' house in Ossining, a few miles north. One morning as Robert was dressing for work in his gray suit, dark blue shirt with the white collar, and polished lace-up shoes,

I wandered down the hall beyond our bedroom toward a shaft of light. There was something on the rug in front of the lacquered door to the Chinese wing. I wandered closer; the something resolved itself into a pile of dog shit.

Standing in the door of the Chinese sitting room, I saw that for the months she had been with us, Maisie had been sneaking off into the south wing to do her business. There were the piles of evidence, among the red porcelain vases and fringed scrolls, on the patterned rug, and against the silk screens. I called Robert, just tying his favorite patterned silk tie and snapping his briefcase shut. Robert always liked to look elegant. When he saw what had happened he started to swear. "Shit," he said. I giggled. He was going to kill Maisie, he said. He sounded as if he meant it. By this time I was too frightened to say anything. I had already cleaned up after so many dogs in my life; Maisie was just one in a string of dogs who couldn't quite make it outdoors.

A long, dark interior hall stretched the length of the house from the Chinese wing on the south end, past our bedroom and Mrs. Vanderlip's empty master bedroom and dressing room, to the nursery on the north. About halfway down its quarter-mile length, it took an abrupt jog to the left for two strides and then continued. A full-length mirror was hung on the wall of the right angle, so that if you were approaching in the dimness from the south it appeared that someone was walking toward you until, with a shock as you reached the mirror, you realized that someone was yourself. Or was it? Often I thought I saw other images in the mirror from a distance, although, of course, when

I got up close it was only the image of an unhappy twenty-four-year-old with a frightened expression and brown hair parted down the middle.

At night when Robert and I fought, we would sometimes, in our rage, end up chasing each other down the corridor. It was in those jerky images in the mirror as we approached in the dark—there were a few wall sconces in the hall, but they hardly lit it—that I saw our marriage was in trouble. There were ghosts at Beechwood. There were doors left mysteriously open or mysteriously locked. Upstairs off the long corridor, where twenty servants had once slept in identical, stark rooms, there was a massive costume room filled with the ball gowns of the past, Chinese robes and Italian silks from the family's many trips abroad, ornate gold gentleman's evening clothes, silver and gold shoes from dances long ago.

THIRTEEN

Beechwood

*T*here were wonderful evenings when guests drove out
from the city and we all sat in the dusky light on the terrace, where the lawns sloped down to the gardens and the
river. Robert mixed martinis in the parlor. My friend Ruthie
came in her convertible, down from Woodstock, New York,
and Robert's friend David came out from the city one night.
We sat on the terrace as daylight faded. It was summer and
hot, and so then we all walked away from the house on the
other side, down past the little house where I had grown up—
I rarely mentioned this to guests—and swam in the pool. We
had it to ourselves. The marble gleamed in the light of the
street lamp over the wall. Later we went back up to the house
for a nightcap. Then we decided it would be a good idea to put
on some records and dance. I remember turning on the lights
in the ballroom. That's all I remember.

When one of the Vanderlip granddaughters got married,

some of the guests came and stayed with us in Beechwood afterwards. It was a great party, with champagne flowing and a
band playing. Robert and I were all dressed up. I noticed that
one of the Schoales boys had fallen in love with one of the
bridesmaids. I ran into a Vanderlip cousin I had had a crush
on when I was a teenager. He was older and a little drunk. I was
prettier now and grown up and a little drunk. I asked him and
his wife to come back up to Beechwood. I remember Robert
wondering angrily why I had done that. I was always inviting
people to come home with us; Robert was sometimes irritated
by this, but he often did it too. After that, though, I don't remember what happened. Not remembering didn't worry me
much. Half the time, most of my friends couldn't even remember what happened during the daylight hours. Remembering was for suckers and squares, I thought. Everyone in my
world made a habit of drinking before dinner and drinking after dinner and forgetting a few things.

Down the curving drive, past the estate's great iron gates,
and up a flight of long steps through a pine grove was the
white Palladian building of the Scarborough School. Bud Stillman had taught my brother there; Ben thought he was a great
teacher. I had gone to see him before I went off to Carbondale.
Now I decided I wanted to teach at the Scarborough School.
Bud Stillman got me a job. In the second autumn we lived in
Beechwood, dressed in the ragged clothes that had survived
the long winter of being just a housewife, I took my place at
the front of the classroom. I still loved to teach. I couldn't say
no to students. I took everyone's advice.

The new headmaster was an ex-athlete gone to chunkiness
who had been a gym master at a much better school. He was a
small-town boy who liked to settle disputes by force. Almost

immediately I was called into his office, the first of many times. In Colorado my students' parents had been far away. Here in Scarborough, where I had grown up, I decided to wage a holy war against the ignorant parents of northern Westchester. I lost.

We were a ragtag bunch of faculty, beginning our careers in a private-school backwater as the sixties came to their terrible end. There was no radio or television at Beechwood. When Robert Kennedy was shot, I sat in the car—in the black Mustang we had bought with my father's money because Robert had always wanted a black Mustang—and listened to the radio most of the night and the next morning.

Beechwood was administered by an elderly Scottish woman named Alice MacKenzie who had been with the Vanderlip family for years. Mrs. MacKenzie was responsible for the maintenance of the place, the deployment of repairmen, and the supervision of Angelo Palumbo. I rarely saw her, but she was watching everything. In order to work at the curved, inlaid desk against the wall of our bedroom, I took a chair that was the right height from one of the bedrooms across the hall. The next day Mrs. MacKenzie was on the phone, gently requesting that I replace Mrs. Vanderlip's Chippendale slipper chair.

For two hundred fifty dollars, Robert and I bought a secondhand red Porsche as a "station car" to have in addition to the Mustang. Beechwood's grandiosity was somehow contagious. When Mrs. MacKenzie once suggested to me that Robert and I probably wouldn't live in Beechwood for another ten years, I was offended. I huffed out of her office. In fact the house was the Vanderlip family white elephant; it was essentially on the market, although there were still members of the family who couldn't bear the idea of their ancestral homestead being torn down or even turned into a think tank or conference center.

They also feared for their own houses, built on the same property, if Beechwood were sold to a developer. While the Vanderlips stalled, we lived there, but I often wondered where we would go afterwards. What could possibly equal the wonderful strangeness, the satisfying eccentricity, the natural beauty of living in such a place? One winter night, as we drank our nightcaps in the front parlor with its silvery wallpaper and Regency sideboards reflecting the light of a blazing fire, Robert told me that he had always dreamed of living in England. "How would we go to England?" I asked. He would like to write a book, Robert said. He had written a few long pieces, one on the Boston police strike, one on the Somme battlefields, one on the Spanish Civil War. The next day he sat down and began work on his book proposal.

FOURTEEN

Parties in
New York City

Sometimes Robert and I drove into the city for a cocktail party or for a sit-down dinner around someone's dining room table. Everyone served chicken baked in sour cream from Craig Claiborne's cookbook; everyone ate garlic bread soaked in butter, and everyone drank before dinner. In those days, at the end of the 1960s and before anyone really understood what had happened to our world, we used to go to parties at Jennifer Hill's apartment. Jennifer had met my parents and become friends with them. She and my mother talked a lot, they even went on trips together, but in those days my father couldn't bear to be in New York City after dark. Jennifer had to settle for me and Robert—who were willing to drive in from the suburbs to New York City at any time for anything that promised to be a good party.

Jennifer was beautiful and had red hair and someone had

left her some money; she had also won prizes for her poetry and written an interesting novel. She had been married to a square investment-banking type named Woody Cohen, but she had left him to soar, to find herself, to go on to better things. When we knew her she had taken up with an Armenian named Lev whom she had met in the bar of a Tad's Steak House. Lev was poor, but he drove a red Cadillac convertible.

Jennifer's apartment was grand and grown-up, and we stood in the wallpapered rooms as the evening settled down over her twelfth-floor gardens and drank scotch. Everyone drank whiskey or gin in those days. Wine was only for dinner. Sometimes we ordered Chinese food—Jennifer always had trouble getting the Chinese delivery boy to take her checks. She always had to call the restaurant to get an okay. "Mrs. Woody Cohen!" she would yell into the telephone, although Woody had moved to Hong Kong. I met Arthur Gregor in that apartment, and Saul Bellow, who wore a little hat and radiated sexual energy. "I have suffered," he said, and then he laughed as if nothing could be funnier.

On my birthday one year, Jennifer handed me a painting by Ruth Kligman, the woman who was in the car with Jackson Pollock when he was killed. Jennifer could have afforded a Pollock, I thought; that she preferred Ruth Kligman was a symbol of her class. The parties were always in the main room of the apartment. In the other rooms were Jennifer's daughter and a tiny, yapping dog. When she was giving parties, Jennifer wore bright Pucci dresses that clung to her curvy figure; when she wasn't giving parties she wore a green T-shirt that said, "A woman without a man is like a fish without a bicycle."

Sometimes when the parties stretched late into the night, bad things happened. I blamed them on Jennifer. She was a wonderful woman, I said, but she was a troublemaker. One night some dark-haired woman friend of someone's made a flagrant pass at my husband, at Robert, and he responded. By then we were all sitting on the hardwood parquet floor, drinking brandy out of little glasses. Late at night, after the dinner wine and the after-dinner drinks and the brandy, we all had a habit of making a long, cool scotch on the rocks. This was a nightcap. The ice clinked in Jennifer's glasses, and New York glittered in the night outside the French doors. The woman whispered in Robert's ear and wrapped herself around him. "I think you're wonderful too," I heard him say.

Sometimes we drove into New York and took Jennifer out to dinner at Orsini's. Orsini's was our favorite restaurant. It was dark and Italian and made us feel glamorous. One night we went there with Chuck Spaulding, and Rudolf Nureyev and Lee Radziwill were standing talking at the bar. It was that kind of place. Chuck Spaulding talked about sailing with the Kennedys. He said that they had always insisted on sailing right through the night; he said sometimes they forgot to navigate. I thought of them, sails set, slicing through the icy waters off the Maine coast, not stopping for anything, unafraid, though the dark sky filled with menace. Robert and I took my parents to Orsini's one night. We were shown to a small table on the second floor—I didn't even know Orsini's had a second floor.

Years later, when Robert and I were divorced and I was alone in New York, someone who was working for her called me and asked me to return the Jackson Pollock painting Jennifer had lent me. I took the Ruth Kligman—a pleasant swirl of yellow on a pink background—out of the closet where it had been for years and walked over to Jennifer's building and handed it to her doorman.

FIFTEEN

Living with the Dead

Robert had been a photographer for a while after he graduated from Harvard. He had hung out with Gary Winogrand at the Central Park Zoo and with Diane Arbus in Greenwich Village, and I took over his old Leica and his Pentax. We outfitted the huge nursery bathroom with darkroom equipment, and I spent days in the dark, watching the images of the river I had photographed appear on the paper in the trays of developer. He taught me how to alter my pictures, how to dodge in and dodge out, using the machines that he had packed in boxes at the end of his first marriage—and that I had unpacked in the nanny's room. I took photographs of the river; of the men in boats, going out at dawn to pull in the shad nets; and the shack village at the bottom of the shale cliff north of Kemeys Cove, where the shad fishermen hung out after the nets were in and it was time to drink.

Beechwood was built along the top of a ridge above the east

bank of the Hudson. The lawns rolled downhill to the west, away from the house, and then flattened out to make the Italian garden with its trellises and archways. Then the land fell away more steeply, to a scrubby cliff that dropped down to the railroad tracks and the river. From every room in the house you could feel the river flowing, deeply flowing at the bottom of the ridge. Its mysterious presence brooded over the valley and over the neighborhood. When it was cold, ice floes bumped their way downstream. When it was hot, the valley seemed to be filled with steam from the roiling, broad water. From the railroad tracks you could see the steep cliffs on the other side, through a summer haze, a world away.

Some nights the heat from the river seemed to roll up the lawn and into our windows like a great, damp beast. At midnight we would walk down to the swimming pool and plunge into the dark water, but by the time we were back in bed we would be covered with sweat. Some of those nights we slept across the hall in Mrs. Vanderlip's old bedroom, where it was slightly cooler, where the pine trees outside the window seemed more bearable than the throbbing water and lawns. Her room hadn't been touched since her death. Once I went to hang something in the closet, and a box of letters fell on the floor. "Thank you for the lovely weekend," I read, in one written in a rolling hand in black ink. "Wallis Windsor." I tucked the box back on the shelf.

Mrs. V.'s bedroom was pale blue—blue had been her color—with a chaise longue, and French doors leading out onto a tiny square terrace at the back of the house. As she got sicker, bars had been installed along the walls in her bathroom to help her get in and out of the tub. Her clothes were still hanging in the closet, her blue bathrobe was on the hook at the back of the bathroom door. It was hard to sleep in her room. The heat was still intense, and I lay there remembering her.

I remembered her formal weekly dancing classes, held in the ballroom and conducted by a Mr. R., a dancing master of the old school. A dozen friends and neighbors would come for dinner and then troop into the ballroom for instructions in the waltz— this always began the evening—and the tango, which always ended it. Mrs. Vanderlip's granddaughter Sarah and I were allowed to attend these evenings. We sat at dinner in the formal dining room and made polite conversation over consommé. I answered questions about school while trying to remember whether to tilt the spoon toward me or away from me.

Then we all gloriously danced. The big Victrola played swing, and the big-band sounds, which echoed off the elaborate friezes on the ceiling, even seemed to make Andromeda, serene in a portrait above the fireplace, smile seraphically. The men, the red-faced bankers and lawyers, would take turns twirling us girls under Mr. R.'s practiced eye. Then, warmed up, they would turn to their wives and away they would go. Mrs. V.'s friend Ralph usually danced with her. I loved those dancing evenings, and as I lay in Mrs. V.'s bed ten years later— although the ten years between the ages of fourteen and twenty-four are surely the longest decade in our lives—I could almost hear the sounds of the big bands wafting up from the great latticed windows of the ballroom through the vitrines of the music room and up the stairs and down the long corridor past the nursery around the corner of the hall.

I didn't wonder if Mrs. Vanderlip was in the room with me on those hot nights I spent tossing and turning on her bed, re- membering the nights I watched as she danced, eternally danced past her bookcases, and past the Steinway grand pianos, and past the great windows and doors that had framed the stage for her grand old-fashioned life. I was uncomfortable, but I didn't know why. Now that I know there are ghosts and that the dead somehow inhabit the places where they lived, lingering among the things that they loved, I imagine that she was there with me on those nights and that her generosity, which had been so unnoticed by me when she was alive, extended somehow to her letting us live in her house.

I think of the way I heard my father coughing in the library of his house in Ossining long after he died; or his footfall on the stairs, coming up from the dining room; or the way he spoke to me once as clearly as if I could hear his voice, and I know that Mrs. Vanderlip was there with us in her house, especially on those dense summer nights. Now I see how much could have gone wrong for us in that huge, haunted place, and I think that maybe she kept us as safe as she could, although that wasn't very safe.

Fighting

*I*n the decade Robert and I knew each other, we lived in five places; we never managed to live anywhere for as long as two years. In the second year we lived at Beechwood, everything began to go wrong. In spite of the knowledge that everything we did would be somehow memorable, in spite of the great bottle of La Tâche '66 we drank there one night or the chilled Château d'Yquem that Robert's friend Darby Bannard brought us one hot Sunday evening, something was out of balance. Somehow my teaching job brought me to life, and that life caused endless trouble in our marriage. In the evenings, Robert and I would settle down peaceably enough for our cocktail hour—on the terrace in warm weather or in the parlor when it was cold. Usually we got through dinner. But by the time I went to serve dessert, we were often fighting desperately, fighting as if our lives depended on it.

We always fought about nothing; we fought about whether

we could afford to buy me a new winter coat, or whether I should fill the car's gas tank in the morning or the afternoon, or whether Robert should work late on Thursday night. But these tiny sources of conflict quickly escalated into ugly power struggles. Soon we were both in a rage. Our anger combined with our drinking created an atmosphere that was more poisonous than the sum of its parts. I once threw a pie plate at Robert's head. He often grabbed me by the shoulders and slammed me against the paneling until my bones made cracking sounds. We chased each other back and forth down the corridors and through the rooms of the great house. When we came, panting, to a stop, we would start over again.

I was a fighter, and I knew how to hurt with words. Fighting with Robert, I felt like a matador, taunting the bull and taunting the bull and taunting the bull until he went crazy. When Robert went crazy, he screamed and lashed out at me. He was a big man with long arms. He liked to tell the story of how Gregory Corso had taught him to box at Cambridge in the 1950s. I would yell, and he would be yelling, and then we would go at each other. I remember a blow and seeing blackness and brightness for a moment. I remember going to teach my eighth-grade English class at the Scarborough School with a black eye. "I walked into a cupboard door," I told everyone. I guess they believed me.

Years later my mother said that my father had not believed me. He sat straight up in bed one morning, she told me, and said, "He's hitting Susie! We have to stop it!" But no one stopped it. No one even talked about it. I don't remember when I first heard the term "domestic violence" used the way we use it now. In those days, in spite of everything that happened in the sixties, I thought that marriage was a private contract between two people. It never occurred to me that Robert had violated this contract by hitting me, and I don't think that, even if it had, many of my friends would have agreed.

Slowly my fights with Robert began to follow a pattern. We would disagree. The fight would begin. I would provoke him: "You do this, and you do this and you do this." His anger would escalate. I would provoke him further. Sometimes he would threaten to kill himself. I would laugh at him. Then he would threaten to kill me; this made me laugh even harder. Finally he'd explode in furious, physical anger. Then, when it was over and he had vented his rage, he would be contrite. I would have won the fight. He would be so sorry. Nothing would be good enough for me. He would beg for my forgiveness. I would give it conditionally. He would be desperate to make it up to me, to heal my wounds, which he had inflicted. How could I put up with a brute like him, he would ask? I loved this mood.

I've written about domestic violence in the past ten years, and I know now that nothing justifies one person hitting another. Even if someone asks you to kill them, you aren't supposed to kill them. Many women are beaten without provocation, and this is a dreadful crime. But to take my black eyes out of context is a failure of understanding. They were just one of the many wounds inflicted in the wild struggle that was our marriage.

We would fight, I would prod Robert and prod him and prod him until this unbearable pressure built up. He would explode. Then he would be sorry. We both had a part in it; it served us both. We were clueless in the world, hungry for recognition, blind to reality, needing to feel whole even if that wholeness was at the expense of someone else's intricate balance.

I began to think that the house was our problem. Of course we felt lost in that huge house, which had been built for other people, I told myself. We needed to follow our own dreams: I used to say that to Dr. Galdston. We needed to strike out and find a life for ourselves that wasn't in the shadow of other people's lives. So I turned against Beechwood and the magic of its arched windows with their views of the lawns and the gardens and the river flowing mysteriously at the bottom of the hill. I turned against the paintings in gold frames and the huge claw-footed bathtub and the graceful way the tile was laid in the walls just at eye level and the curving staircases and the columned terraces. I turned against the many ways in which we had tried to live up to the house, the elaborate charts we had kept on the wall to record the wines we had drunk there, the flower arrangements, the dinner parties. All that was history. We would go to the place we called Yerp. We would leave Dr. Galdston, who was still kissing me on the mouth and feeling my breasts, and who pretended he didn't know what I was talking about when I protested. "My other patients are loving people," he would say, his face lighting up with an approval I longed for. We would leave behind our terrible fights. We would have adventures together. We would find a new life.

Expatriates

*I*n the summer of 1969, we read about Chappaquiddick in
the Spanish newspapers we bought outside the café in
Palma where we went to drink Campari before lunch. We saw
the moon landing on a tiny black-and-white television set in a
bar in Deya. We began our new life in Spain because we had
friends there, and because the idea of a summer in Spain, the
drive north over the Pyrenees in the fall, and the winter in
London seemed irresistible. In Deya we rented the top floor of
a house with a view of the endless sea. We lived above a family
with three small children and a puppy. Robert had been talking about having children. God sent this family to change his
mind. They were an academic family, and my first real exposure to expatriates and the life Americans lead abroad. Driven
by the glamour of the idea—He took the family to live on an
island in Spain! They ran off to the south of France!—they are
often forced to live in their heads. Only the view from outside,

the voices of their friends back in Senappy, New Jersey, jealously gossiping at the Rotary dinner, can make the discomfort of exile worthwhile. It was no fun to live in Majorca, really. The food was bad, conditions were primitive, the great Spanish cathedrals and paintings were far away, the great Spanish novels already translated. There was the spectacular landscape and the way a dollar was worth a lot of pesetas, but that wasn't why any of us were there.

The Cala—a rocky cove and tiny beach bounded by two promontories—was the town's principal meeting place. In the afternoons there were chess games under a thatch roof. At meals there was fresh fish in a restaurant a few steps up from the beach. Every afternoon Robert Graves appeared with his entourage: a few spectacularly beautiful girls in bikinis; a few young Englishmen with slicked-back hair and ruddy faces. Graves wore a wide-brimmed hat. He was an old man then, but still tall and limber, and as his group watched in admiration he would climb out onto the rocks, picking his way upwards like a rock climber, and then turn and plunge into the glistening dark blue sea.

Once when Robert and I had walked out on one of the rocky peninsulas near our house, fighting because we were always fighting, we ran into Graves. We all sat and looked out at the water—there was nothing to see but the sun turning it blue and golden and deep purple. Graves held my hand and sang a song in Latin. "Always the bridesmaid, never the bride," he sang. We all laughed. The fight was over. Then he clambered back along the rocks to have dinner prepared by his wife, Beryl.

My parents, my brother Fred, and my cousin Ann came to visit us in Deya. I had told them it was beautiful. They hated it. I had checked them into a charming local pension owned by one of Graves' sons. My mother got sick. The minute she could travel she and Fred took off for Madrid, where they checked into the Ritz. At least, my mother said, they had decent towels. Back in Deya, my father limped angrily along the Cala. Nothing could cheer him up. My mother wrote to say she was leaving Madrid and going to Rome. Robert and I went to meet her. We stayed at the Hassler Hotel. (My father stayed in Deya.) In four days we spent half the money we had set aside for a year. Before he went back to New York, my father wrote us a check.

For lunch, back in Deya, I simmered vegetables on a hot plate, and then threw in a few canned sardines or olives. I flattened the cans and buried them with the compost and our broken wine bottles in a hole at the end of the garden. Some friends of ours lent us a different house, a series of three big white rooms a half-hour hike up the cliff at the entrance to town. It was one of the most beautiful places I've ever seen. High up in the olive groves, we looked down on the cliffs breaking away to the sea. Hawks flew below us. It was perfectly quiet.

A few days before we left Deya, Robert began to have intestinal cramps. Robert didn't take such symptoms lightly. In our life together there were many emergency calls to doctors and late-night trips to hospitals. He had a certain quality of broodiness that I came to know meant he thought he was dying.

We went to the local physician. He examined Robert with great fanfare. Robert was fine, he finally pronounced, but he had a swollen liver. Everything would be all right if he didn't drink for a few weeks. How many weeks? Robert asked. Oh, two or three weeks, the doctor said. "You don't mean wine too?" I asked. Wine too, the little doctor said in Spanish, and he shook his head as if to predict great unhappiness if his instructions weren't followed. Later, Robert was very angry at me for asking about wine.

At any rate, I remember that we both thought this was a barbaric prescription. It didn't seem possible to drive through France without drinking, anymore than it would have seemed possible to drive through France without gasoline. Didn't the doctor understand that we were serious about wine? That we had devoted a great deal of time and energy to the study of the great vineyards and their ambrosial produce? By the time we had driven through Andorra and reached the walled town of Carcassonne in the southernmost corner of France, Robert was drinking again, drinking red wine in half bottles because the doctor had said he shouldn't drink and half bottles didn't really count.

Our trip was gruesome. I wanted to stop everywhere. Robert, who was trying not to drink and drinking anyway, wanted to stop nowhere. At a hotel in Les Eyzies called the Cro-Magnon, where Stone Age cave drawings were right there in the hallway because the hotel was built into a cave, we both got sick. Coughing and wheezing, we stumbled through the damp prehistoric caves of the Dordogne. Our guides held up lanterns so that we could see the horses and other wild creatures men and women had carved at the dawn of time.

In London, we found a roomy flat in a shabby house on Westbourne Terrace near the Bayswater Road. Robert settled down to write his book in a tiny study that had been built over the kitchen—the room hung like a treehouse from the high ceiling. Almost every weekday morning I left our flat and took the Number 15 bus to Fleet Street, where I worked at *Queen* magazine. A friend of ours from Deya had been hired as the editor. There was no office for me, so I was temporarily installed in the office of Anne Barr, an editor who was on vacation. It looked to me as if she had been on vacation for a long time. Her office was piled with manuscripts, many of them from established writers.

I started in on answering the dozens of eager accompanying letters. Many of the writers replied by return mail. Often their articles were excellent; soon we were running them in the magazine. Within a few weeks I had become the articles editor. For lunch, a group of us would troop down Fleet Street to El Vinos, and often by the time we were done it was late afternoon and I had to get the bus home. It was my job, after all, to put supper on the table, to make sure that Robert had three meals a day, to pick up the cleaning and his shirts.

In the evening, or on weekends, Robert and I went down a few blocks on the Bayswater Road to The Swan, or across Praed Street to the Plow and Stars. We loved the British pubs with their wood paneling and their comfortable seats and the rosy glow cast out into the street through mullioned windows. We loved the rituals of off hours and the way the publican would line up the beers at the last call. There was always a drunk muttering in the corner. There was always a couple embracing on the banquette, there was always tobacco smoke and the smell of leather, and there was always a dog peeing against the bar.

It's true that I have had three marriages that ended, but these days I don't remember them as failures. I had three amazing marriages to three exceptional men. In each case, I got married assuming that marriage would last our lifetimes. Two of my husbands helped support me financially while I got my own balance—a gift which is always worth more than the actual money—two of them are the fathers of my children, my children who are at the center of my life. All three of my husbands were writers and editors, and all three taught me to write. It is a great privilege to learn by watching, of course; but each of my husbands had an active hand in editing and shaping both my prose and my ideas about prose. The first of those writing lessons was that winter in London. At an editor's request I had written a small piece for *Queen* about the Italian cartoonist Dino Buzzatti. Writing the piece took all day, and I was quite proud of it. The editor, to my surprise and dismay, was not impressed. I took the piece home to show to Robert; I knew that he would recognize my talent. He read the piece and pulled a chair out for me next to him. "Let me show you how we do this," he said.

My best friend was Ruthie Elias, a Colorado Rocky Mountain School student during my time there, who had come to live in England after a stint at Bennington College. She was living in a flat in Little Venice and having an affair with a married man with three children. She said that they were in love; they saw each other at least every day. On the door of her flat, four steep flights up from the street, was a hand lettered sign. "Richard, I love you forever," it said. Above her bed there was a picture of her dancing with him.

I had read enough Iris Murdoch to think that Ruthie was probably kidding herself. She was always short of money. Odd friends from New York or Bennington or other people's friends were always camping out on her floor. One of them gave us all Christmas presents she had stolen from the best stores in Piccadilly.

Though they sometimes drove her crazy, Ruthie couldn't say no to this parade of ragtag Americans. She was a child, and in many ways she became Robert's and my child—although her parents were plenty worried over on the other side of the Atlantic.

Ruthie was a great cook and was always whipping up wonderful dinners for groups of hungry friends. One night she called us in tears—she had cooked dinner for some people who had just called to cancel. Robert and I rushed right over. We watched hungrily as she expertly poured heavy cream into a skillet with chops and squeezed out a press of aromatic garlic. We ate hungrily too; it was delicious. As we sat there feasting, Robert, usually a reserved man, decided to sing Ruthie one of his favorite songs—a ditty he had written called "The Martyr Song."

"M is for the mother that you're made of," he started, "A is for the aches you've borne untold. R is for the roses that adorn your shrine . . ." As he got to the end of the song, "R is for that rat out in the cold," a dark-haired man bounded into the kitchen. It was the man in the photograph above the bed.

By now, thirty years later, Ruthie and Richard have been married a long time. In the meantime I've been divorced and remarried twice and separated again. Richard is a lord now, and a famous architect who has changed the face of the world. Ruthie is famous too, and when I call her at a hotel I have to ask for Lady Rogers. I went shopping with them at Issey Miyake recently. They are so close and have been together so long that they speak a private language. As they flipped through the clothes, I could see that Richard, usually a man of a few benign words, was keeping up a running commentary on style and color, his mouth close to Ruthie's ear. Then she'd try something on. He could tell what she thought without her saying anything.

The bus rides to Fleet Street were grimmer as the winter wore on. Down Oxford Street past blocks of empty office buildings we trundled, then back again from Fleet Street and across London toward the distant Westbourne Terrace. Waiting in the bus queue in my raincoat, I was often cold. The English loved to wait in line. I hated to wait in line. Robert was writing huge pieces of his book, but he could never put them together. Instead, when the time came to turn something in, he would tear it apart and obsessively write and rewrite. It was never good enough; it was never done. At the start of the summer, his old boss called and offered him a job.

The time just before you leave is often the sweetest time. When we had bought our plane tickets for our return home in July, a friend lent us his Morgan convertible, one of those cars with a leather strap over the hood and a top you could disassemble and store in the boot, and we headed for the World War I battlefields in northern France. Robert had urged me to read everything I could about World War I: Graves, Sassoon, Liddell Hart, and Wilfred Owen and David

Jones. We stood at the top of the rise near Bapaume where Sassoon had stood and saw what was left of the trenches. We tramped through Belleau Wood and saw the stunted tree where both Graves and Jones had written of a terrible scene, a German soldier and a British soldier simultaneously bayoneting each other to death.

There was something infinitely moving about the bravado of the Great War, the courage of men who had no idea that they were walking into the end of the world, men who went over the top in a soccer formation in their Oxford team shirts, men who were happy to die for God and country, who believed that it was a sweet and decorous thing to die for England, as the poet Wilfred Owen so bitterly wrote in "Dulce et Decorum Est." We had dinner at the Godbert in Amiens, where the French generals had eaten, and then the German generals and then afterwards the French generals again and finally the Americans.

We saw the endless fields of wheat, spattered with red poppies, the rows that couldn't grow straight because of the carnage that had once been there—as if the blood of all those young men had permanently scarred the earth. We bought baguettes and local wine and charcuterie and picnicked at the edges of the fields, using the car's fenders as a table. Then we drove back up to the coast, crossed the Channel, went through the amazingly green fields of Kent, and packed to go home.

We moved back in with my parents in Ossining, and Robert started commuting to New York. I quickly found us a little house for rent in Armonk, and we moved in, putting an old box spring from my parents' attic in the living room, along with a cheap beanbag chair as our furniture. A creaky bed in the master bedroom came with the house. My parents lent us their old kitchen table for a dining room table, and we collected a rickety assortment of straight-backed chairs. When Robert's daughters visited on weekends, they slept in the attic on mattresses. When guests came, they perched on the box spring, which I had covered with a red Hudson's Bay blanket, or shifted uncomfortably on the straight chairs. I was at the end of my twenties; Robert was almost forty years old.

By getting married, I believed, I had earned the right to never have to work again. My London job had been more fun than work. At the little house in Armonk it soon became clear that Robert's salary wouldn't pay our expenses. I had to get a job. Seething with resentment, I began preparing résumés. I had taught for three years at that point, but I had no real teaching credentials, and it was already October. I applied for a job in the public relations department of Continental Can, but in my heart I thought I could get hired at the *Reader's Digest*, where my Uncle Joe Hotchkiss worked. *Reader's Digest* editors took me out to lunch. I edited a book for them as a test. More editors took me out to lunch. "We don't want to lose this one," one of them said in my hearing. But instead I got a stiff letter saying they didn't have a job to offer me at this time.

Financially we felt desperate, a familiar desperation. Living abroad had drained our resources. In the afternoons, before going to get Robert at the White Plains station, I wove macramé belts and chokers, which I gave on consignment to the local sporting goods store. I went to the state unemployment office in White Plains and got stuck in the elevator. They didn't have a job for me either. I applied for a job at the newspaper in White Plains. The editor held up a sheaf of papers.

"These are applications from experienced journalists," he said. "Why are you here?"

One afternoon I got a call from Harry Donsky, the editor of the *Tarrytown Daily News*. I went to see him. His office was a tiny room with three desks crowded into it. Behind that room was a composing room, where I could see men in overalls pouring and thumping. A white-haired woman was hunched over a typewriter in the corner, chain-smoking, pounding at the keys, and talking on the telephone all at the same time. A younger woman with dark teased hair and chewing a wad of gum sat in the next room, also talking on the telephone. "Can you start Monday?" Harry Donsky asked. He was a gray-haired man in an Eisenhower sweater. He wore a blue striped tie that looked as if it had come with his blue striped shirt.

"Sure," I said. On the way home, because I would soon be bringing home a paycheck of a hundred dollars a week, I stopped off at the Art of Wine, a store in Pleasantville, and bought a case of Pouilly-Fuissé and a very reasonably priced case of Pomerol '69.

We were home again, but our lives would never be the same. For one thing, we were both drinking more all the time. It was harder to drive home from parties in New York at night, and more and more gruesome to get up and go to work in the morning. Perhaps more importantly, I had found a job I loved. I had never really understood the pleasures of work before; I had had jobs, but I had never had power. In our marriage, Robert had all the power. Now that began to change.

EIGHTEEN

Journalism

Although we couldn't admit it, our great dream—Robert's of being a writer and mine of being a writer's wife— was over. We had awakened not in a glamorous life in the south of France with Robert growing a beard like the great Papa Hemingway and exclaiming over the quality of the local wine I served him at lunch, but in a small white suburban house in the woods at the unfashionable edge of Westchester County.

We were both disappointed; we never mentioned this. We continued to talk about our life as if it were a great adventure, although we lived with no furniture and a dwindling budget, and our weekends with Robert's children became less frequent and more difficult. With breathtaking speed, it seemed, we had gone from being a promising, talented young couple to a couple of has-beens. Robert had a diminished job, and I, at least at first, had no job at all. We had few possessions and not enough money. I threw our bills into a shoe box and forgot them as long as I could.

Even though we felt like losers, we considered it a point of pride to keep up some kind of appearances. We still had dinner parties—guests balanced their plates of boeuf bourguignon on their laps as they teetered at the edge of the box spring. We still spent all our extra money on wine and kept our meticulous wine log. We still celebrated the end of the day with a few scotches. This was the time, after the first few sips of that mellow fire, that it all seemed worthwhile. It was our evening drink that made the whole crazy disappointment seem like a fascinating figure in life's great tapestry.

The first Monday morning I walked up the dingy stairs and into the tiny rooms of the *Tarrytown Daily News* there was already a crisis in motion. Sandy Pelosi, who usually covered the police, had called in sick. I was dispatched to the Irvington, Tarrytown, and North Tarrytown—the tri-village area—police stations for my first encounter with a police blotter. In those days the police blotter, the daily log kept by the officer at the desk, was the carefully guarded beating heart of the community—everything was on it from a fire started at the railroad station by a prominent citizen's son, to a domestic fistfight in the richest part of town, to a squirrel coming in the bathroom window at the Bienick residence on Elm Road and frightening the Bienick's housekeeper.

At first the policemen treated me like a pet girl. I was cute, and they were in control. Slowly I gained their trust, and I learned how to read the blotter upside down. I found out that if I made a few calls before "doing the cops" I could sometimes surprise them into admissions, too. Irvington, Tarrytown, and North Tarrytown were sleepy little Hudson River hamlets on the surface. Most of their acreage was filled with residential rows of white frame houses, shaded by oaks and maples, leading down to a broad row of shops on a main street, in each case called Main Street.

North Tarrytown wasn't quite like the other Hudson River towns. At the end of Main Street in North Tarrytown was the twenty-eight-acre General Motors factory. The men who fished the Hudson said they could tell what color the cars were being painted that day by what came up in their nets. General Motors usually refused to respond to reporters from the *Tarrytown Daily News,* but the bars on Beekman Avenue filled up after work with the men who worked for GM—men who were happy to tell a pretty girl everything they knew.

At the other end, North Tarrytown abutted Pocantico Hills, the thousands of acres that were privately held by the Rockefeller family and which included an entire village and a country church with Matisse and Chagall windows, all owned by the family, and Kykuit, the huge Beaux Arts country house of Nelson Rockefeller, then the governor of New York State. Nelson's brother Laurence owned the land to the north, and the brothers had helped promote the Hudson River Expressway, a highway to be built on landfill running along the water, which had finally, after much struggle, been stopped by a coalition of environmentalists and concerned residents of the river communities, including my parents.

Between General Motors and the Rockefellers there were plenty of opportunities for a newspaper reporter to find out things no one wanted in the paper. But what made the *Tarrytown Daily News* such a wonderful place to work was something more ordinary than those two story possibilities: it was the ebb and flow of human quirkiness and eccentricity that

characterizes small-town life. It was the tidbits picked up at
the bars after the paper shut, or the comment heard at a tag
sale up on Benedict Avenue, or a lead from Gert, the woman
who ran the coffee wagon in a repainted school bus across
from the paper, or the observations of an off-duty cop who
happened to be in a bar on Saint Patrick's Day—the day all the
bars served huge mugs of green beer. It was everything from
the angry builders at the zoning board meetings, to the man
who jumped off the Tappan Zee Bridge after losing his job, to
the cemetery worker at the Sleepy Hollow Cemetery who im-
molated himself on the biggest mausoleum in the place.

Working out of a shabby building, with limited resources,
Harry Donsky had assembled a group of reporters who were
ready to take on anything. Doing my job, I felt the combination of excitement and mastery that I know well now, but that
I had rarely felt before. Robert and the house in Armonk
seemed to fade, the color literally leaching out of them in my
mind's eye, and become remote and uninteresting. During the
drive to work in the morning—I left the house just after 6
A.M.—I would begin to feel that I was coming alive. On the
way home, often late at night, after a school board meeting or
night court session, I would write the next day's story in my
head, picking over the events of the evening to find the most
important things. I wasn't interested in hearing about Robert's
work anymore. Instead of getting home for our drink, I was
often held up in one of the bars on Beekman Avenue, chatting
with a source, a colleague, or just anyone who wanted to talk.
Our dinners became more and more perfunctory, although I
often stopped off at the Art of Wine on the way home—it was
usually open late.

One night at a school board meeting I noticed a group of

elegant, dark-haired men and women in evening clothes who had come to speak. They sat silently while the usual small-town politicians had their usual temper tantrums. Buzzy Harrod, I remember, actually pounded on the Formica-topped school table when someone suggested a tax increase.

As the travesty ended, one of the well-dressed men stepped forward. They were Cubans, representing the large Cuban community in Tarrytown, they explained. They had been driven to America by Castro and Castro's socialism. They wanted to petition the school board for some English-as-a-second-language classes for their children. I spoke to them after the meeting; they invited me and my family for dinner. I quickly became fascinated with these Cubans, many of them wealthy or successful professionals who were busy renovating the run-down houses on Hamilton Place and Franklin Street and taking over some of the local businesses.

In the end I fell in love with all the Cubans in general, for their work ethic and their good looks and their memories and their great sadness, and with one of the Cubans in particular. Harry Donsky suggested I write a series about them, family by family, and I did. He slugged it "Havana on Hudson." It won a prize. In the meantime, a friend of my parents' mentioned that the Rockefellers were making preparations to sell off most of their vast land holdings—including the entire village of Pocantico Hills—keeping only a 150-acre compound for themselves. "Absolutely not," the Rockefeller public relations woman told me. I kept her chatting on the telephone for a while. "You're too smart for the *Tarrytown Daily News*," she finally said.

Later that night, after Robert and I had our cocktails, I sat down and wrote a letter to the Metro Editor of *The New York*

Times, asking if they would be interested in using me as a stringer. A stringer is a freelance reporter who covers sources the newspaper can't reach or can't afford to reach. I mentioned that there was a Rockefeller story brewing.

One afternoon in the morgue of the newspaper, a dusty interior room with bound volumes on sagging shelves, where I was reading through the clips on the Rockefellers and the history of Pocantico Hills, Harry Donsky came and sat on the little stool we used to reach the high shelves. "What's up?" he asked. I told him about my letter to the *Times* and about the way they had asked me to cover the story. Since we were an afternoon paper, I explained to him, we would always have the story first. He had grounds to fire me. Instead, he smiled and put a hand on my shoulder for a second. "Blow us out of the water!" he said, and he laughed.

Other things happened in the two years I worked in Tarrytown. A particular Cuban set about seducing me. It took him a long time. There were lunches at the Hilton and lunches at the Cuban restaurant on Main Street, called the Ninth Inning because Cubans loved baseball. He had to convince me that we were in love, and he did. We slept together a few times, in my house in Armonk on the bed Robert and I had inherited with the place. It was awful when he was there and painful when he left.

The day the Rockefeller story broke was a day he was supposed to be there with me. "We need time together," he would say, as he rushed off or I ran late for an interview. This was to have been our third afternoon together. I left the newspaper and eked out the story through phone interviews, one ear cocked toward the driveway where, I hoped, any second I would hear his yellow Oldsmobile crunch in on the gravel. Later he said he had tried to call me but my line was busy.

The Rockefeller story ran in Tarrytown and then in the *Times* with someone else's by-line. While the story was closing, and the facts were being checked, someone at the *Times* told the Rockefellers who their stringer was. "Oh, was that supposed to be kept quiet?" the *Times* editor asked. The Rockefeller public relations woman had been right. I thought I was too smart for the *Tarrytown Daily News*. I let her believe I was writing for the local paper when in fact my heart was set on *The New York Times*. The next day I was summoned to Kykuit. I drove through the great gates, which shut behind me, and down a long curved drive. Deep gravel crunched under the tires as I turned in through a second gate. I pulled the car up next to buildings made of heavy stones. A green pickup truck was parked outside with a man sitting in the driver's seat who motioned me indoors with a curt nod. I waited in a small room for a long time; the windows were covered with ivy growing outside. The Rockefeller public relations woman finally came into the room and shut the door behind her. She didn't even sit down. "You lied to me," she said. "Yes," I said, "I did." I sat captive in a hard chair and listened to my heart beat and felt my stomach sink. Let me tell you, if I were ever going to stop writing, I would have stopped right then.

NINETEEN

San Francisco

*I*n the winter, Robert was offered a high-paying job by Nick Charney and John Veronis, two publishing entrepreneurs who had bought the moribund *Saturday Review* from Norman Cousins and planned to relocate it to San Francisco. I told Robert I couldn't go; he said he would go without me. But when the time came on a Friday afternoon for Robert to go, I was struck by waves of panic. I took him to the airport, unable to control my weeping. He was touched. I drove home to the little house, sobbing with loneliness. I had a drink. The sky began to darken. Nightfall. I called a few friends; no one was home. I had another drink. I decided that I should get on a plane and join Robert in San Francisco.

I remember my first night there, the eucalyptus-scented air and the sound of the foghorns. Robert and I slept in a four-poster in a house on Cherry Street. The piney woods of the Presidio were across the street. On Monday morning, after I had been in San Francisco one day, I called my new boss at the newspaper. I had been promoted out of Tarrytown to White Plains a few weeks before I left. "I'm in San Francisco," I said to this editor. "When are you coming back?" he said. "Never," I said.

For the first few months we were in San Francisco we went to parties and planned fancy lunches in private rooms and spent money. There were parties in huge Victorian houses in Pacific Heights that looked like funeral parlors, and parties on boats in San Francisco Bay and parties in famous people's houses. Soon I felt as if we knew everyone in San Francisco. At a party at I. F. Stone's sister Judy's house, we met Warren Hinckle and his wife, Denise; they stalked in like royalty, which they were, in a way. Warren wore a crimson velvet suit and silk tie, and his long black hair was pulled back behind an eye patch. He was the city's celebrity homeboy, a man who had grown up in San Francisco and who was famous enough as a journalist to be on the front page of *The New York Times*. In San Francisco they took stuff like that personally.

But by Christmas it became clear that Charney and Veronis didn't have enough money to support their own habits, and that one of their most expensive habits was the *Saturday Review*. There were still parties, huge bashes at the remodeled warehouse where worried editors huddled in corners over shrimp and champagne to discuss which sections had been cut, who was going home. There were dinners at the fancy houses in Sausalito and Mill Valley other editors had rented or bought for their families, dinners where heads rolled, and men who had just eaten oysters and caviar vomited it up in the marble bathrooms.

Coming to San Francisco had been our chance to become, again, the promising young couple we once had been. Every time we moved, every time the job changed or the house changed or the country changed, I was suffused with this mad hope that somehow this new start would be different, that somehow we would begin to build something that would amount to something instead of fizzling out and leaving us to wait for the next chance at a new start. As the hope drained out of our San Francisco adventure, everything began going wrong—again. The roof leaked. Our dogs got sick. We fought all the time. Of course we drank wine at lunch and scotch or martinis in the evening and beer in between. Sometimes I drank so much that I forgot what had happened the night before—again. Sometimes Robert drank so much that he fell asleep during dinner, or said something I thought was rude to an editor who had power over him.

If you had suggested that there was any connection between what we drank and what was happening to us, what always seemed to be happening to us, Robert and I would both have been amazed. We drank the way everyone did, or so we believed. As we loaded our car to drive back to New York after the *Saturday Review* went into Chapter Eleven, two unemployed people, now getting on in years, once more headed for my parents' house, we had no idea why this had happened to us.

My marriage to Robert was over so many times that when it finally was over I think we were both relieved. It was over in Amiens, France, when I realized that I couldn't write his book and that he wouldn't be able to write it either. It was over in Armonk when I went to work for the newspaper and fell in love with the job and then fell in love with another man. It was over when I realized I didn't want to go to California with

Robert; it was over when I went anyway. It was over in Elko, Nevada, on our way back to New York when our shocks needed to be replaced. It was especially over when Warren Hinckle came to New York the next summer without his wife, Denise, and took me out for dinner without Robert, and made me laugh.

Warren After Dark

*A*t first my connection to Warren was so overpowering that it seemed to have come from another world, a previous incarnation. I wondered if we were, somehow, brother and sister. Perhaps my father had met Warren's mother during the war on his way to the Philippines. I dreamed up impossible scenarios like this because that's what my bond with Warren felt like.

It didn't happen all at once. At first I was frightened of Warren, with his wild reputation and his quickness to say exactly what wasn't expected. It was 1972, and he was famous; famous for turning *Ramparts* into a magazine that unmasked the CIA's recruiting techniques, and famous for his Chicago hijinks in 1968, and, by this time, famous for being a famous radical. He had folded his latest magazine after issues were seized at the United States border by the Canadian Royal Mounted Police, and, at age thirty-four, he was working on a memoir entitled *If You Have a Lemon, Make Lemonade.*

The night it happened, a year after we first met, in the middle of a New York City summer, his wife was far away in California with the kids, and my husband was in Boston because the only job he could get after we came back from California was in Boston. Warren and I were sitting there, at one of the big round tables at Elaine's restaurant, with some of the people who used to go there: Lacey Fosburgh and Milos Forman and Tom Buckley. It was one of those nights when people just give themselves over to the heat and sit around glowing with sweat and drinking gin and tonics, and we had just had dinner with Warren's friends Ann and Maxwell Geismar and it turned out that Max had taught my mother at Sarah Lawrence and that Ann had met my father once and the Geismars had a dog and Warren had a dog and I had a dog and my parents had a dog, and suddenly everything seemed to fall into place in a fuzzy, meant-to-be sort of way.

In that moment, the moment long after the waiter had first come to our table and announced that Elaine would like to buy us an after-dinner drink, that moment long after I had stopped counting my gin and tonics, that moment when I was about to switch to stingers, I knew that Warren and I had a true bond which would last until the end of time. Maybe I knew right then that bond would be at the emotional center of two decades of my life, that it would be there even when Warren went back to his wife and little girls in California, and I drove up to Boston to join Robert for a weekend on the Cape; that it would be there even when I left Robert and went to work at *Newsweek;* that it would be there even when I married Calvin and had my first child, Sarah; that it would be there, waiting, when my marriage to Calvin came apart; that it would be there even then.

San Francisco, with Warren there, became my Mecca, my goal of goals, the place where I aimed my personal and professional life. I was living on East 74th Street, but I lived for the telephone calls and for my trips west. I sold San Francisco stories to New York editors and then went to California to research them, and to see Warren. Often, though, when I got there, I felt trapped. I would get off the plane and walk into the eucalyptus bright air, take a cab to the hotel and wait for Warren. Loving Warren was waiting for Warren. Soon my exhilaration began to wear off.

Warren had told me about Virginia City, a town near Reno, Nevada, where the riches of the Comstock Lode had exploded at the end of the nineteenth century, making it the richest town in the world, a haven for brilliant Victorian architecture, a meeting place of Presidents, and, of course, the home of the brilliant newspaper, the *Territorial Enterprise,* where Mark Twain and Ambrose Bierce had worked as reporters. Warren said he was going to buy the *Territorial Enterprise* and we would both go work there. I sold the idea of a Virginia City story to Oliver Jensen at *American Heritage,* and headed to the airport.

Warren was too busy with his wife and children to come with me, so I drove alone to Virginia City. I got there just at nightfall and checked into the Silver Dollar Hotel. The town appeared deserted; it was March, but the hotel's Christmas decorations were still up. Sometime in the night I was awakened by the sounds of a couple making love next door. I looked east in the flat steely light that was beginning to seep up from the horizon and thought about the fact that there was nothing but emptiness for thousands of miles. I left the hotel and walked out into the gray dawn. The mine shafts were crumbling and dangerous, the houses all seemed to be falling down. A stray dog clattered over a garbage pail behind the hotel and pawed through its contents.

I had come to interview people, but by noon it had begun to snow hard. I knew that if I didn't get out of Virginia City, right then, I would die. I made my excuses and drove down the mountain, far exceeding the speed limit. I sped through Reno, then with a sigh of relief, turned west on Route 80 and started over Donner Pass. It was snowing harder. The first chain station was lit up. Do not proceed without chains, signs warned. I proceeded without chains. I had to get out of there.

The snowfall increased, and soon I was guiding the car only with the help of the median divider, which I could barely see through the snow. Powder streamed past me as the car bumped ahead. I passed another booth where all the other traffic seemed to have stopped. The pass was closed, the sign said. I just kept on driving. The car began to shimmy and snow thumped against the doors. As the unplowed drifts deepened, the car slowed to a halt. Reluctantly, I turned around. I drove back into Reno and appeared in the office of a friend of my parents, a nice man named Ted Nash. Who knows what he thought, finding me there, shaking with anxiety. He bought me a drink and got on the telephone. Soon the pass was open again, and I set out, with chains on this time. It was nighttime by the time I cleared the pass and drove on down through Baxter and Colfax toward Auburn and Sacramento and that golden, shimmering city by the bay. I remember it now as vividly as if it was yesterday, the lights in the valley below me and the clear road ahead; I felt as if I could fly.

William Styron wrote an unfriendly review of Max Geismar's book on Henry James the summer after that—the summer after Warren and I fell in love—and Warren decided to exact some revenge on behalf of his friend. We would send Styron a box of dog shit, Warren announced one evening. My friend Linda Greenhouse had come for dinner. I had met her when I was working at the *Tarrytown Daily News* and she was working for the Westchester bureau of *The New York Times*—she *was* the Westchester bureau of *The New York Times*—and Warren dragooned us both into collecting the dog shit. He produced a Bonwit Teller bag and proceeded to scour the sidewalk.

Linda laughed, but she didn't help. Then Warren said we had to go out to the Geismars' for dinner. Whatever Warren said to do, I did. We got in the car with the bag of dog shit and two six-packs of beer. I drove. Linda sat next to me. "Give me a beer," I said. I remember the way she gingerly took the beer out of the carton. I remember her nail tapping on the surface of the can before she opened it. She put her seat belt on. I could tell she thought we were insane.

The next night, at my parents' house in Ossining, we boxed the dog shit we had collected. We laid everything out on the dining room table and created a family ceremony, as if we were wrapping Christmas presents. Warren said it was important to do it correctly because my brothers had never sent dog shit before. My father was away somewhere teaching and having affairs and drinking himself to death. My mother hardly ever came downstairs. The next morning we mailed the package at the post office. Warren said how wonderful it would be when the redolent parcel arrived at the Styrons' and at first they thought it was some kind of exotic cheese—only to discover it was dog shit. That would teach Styron, he said. I've met William Styron at parties a few times since then. I used to think he might not remember getting that package from Ossining, but now I wonder how easy it is to forget something like that. I never talk to him for long.

TWENTY-ONE

Opposites

$\mathcal{M}$y brother Ben has a maxim he calls "the rule of contrary." What he means is that often when people say something, they mean the opposite. This is true of everything from a kind of knee-jerk reaction like "I love your haircut," which is often code for "what did you do to your hair?" to the "I love you" a man says to a woman he is trying to mollify, or the "I love you" a woman says to a man she is trying to possess. The rule of opposites applies to much more than just the way people talk to each other. It's an integral part of the way the universe operates, a kind of contrary nature of circumstance that makes it almost sure that whatever we expect will not happen and whatever we least expect will happen. I call this the perversity of God.

By the time Robert and I were divorced, I was already in trouble with Warren. We fought, and Warren was a brilliant fighter. In the end I always said that Warren knew how to make war but he didn't know how to make love, but that was years later. Robert always did what I wanted, and I complained that was boring. In fact it had a kind of deadening effect on him as his will got smaller and smaller under the pressure of what I wanted and needed. Warren never did anything I wanted, and that was a problem too. He didn't leave his wife when I wanted him to. He was never on time. He didn't call when he said he would. All this tied me to him more. The feelings I had when Warren let me down, even then, the feelings of abandonment and despair and yearning, so much yearning, seemed to me to be feelings engendered by a great passion. The feelings were so painful—even after a few drinks, even when I diluted my morning coffee with brandy, even when I spent afternoons sipping Diet Coke spiked with framboise because it seemed such a sophisticated drink—that I knew they must come from my heart. That was the one thing Warren did that I wanted; he agreed that we had a great love, that we weren't like other people, that our love transcended the silly lives led by most people we knew.

In college we read in Plato's *Republic* that everything has an ideal form. Plato thought that the things we think we know are actually twice removed from that ideal. In Plato, we see shadows thrown by puppets that only represent the ideal. Is the chair I sit in just a shadow of an ideal chair, and this book that I'm writing and you are reading a shadow of some ideal version of this book? In my life I can see that my father played the part of this ideal form, the original man in my life, and that every man I've been involved with has somehow been a shadow of his giant figure. Not that my father was so ideal—he too may have been one of Plato's puppets. Nevertheless, I see him in every man I love.

I met Calvin on a rainy afternoon at the end of the summer of 1975. My father and I had driven to lunch at the Ettlingers', some old friends in Rockland County. I was introduced to this man, but I didn't catch his name. He was drinking Kir—white wine with a shot of cassis. I drank my white wine straight; that way my glass could be refilled without it seeming as if I was having another drink. In those days I had nothing but contempt for Kir drinkers. I made fun of this man's Kir; I explained to him that Kir drinkers were careful people, moderate people whose desperate faddishness was exceeded only by their ignorance of wine. He laughed and sat down next to me. I could see his chic wife in the shadows across the room—she was the kind of woman who could wear a belt outside of her sweater and still look thin. I could tell that she never made fun of her husband.

He and I talked about *Newsweek*—he said he had worked there—and about San Francisco and about Warren. He was an attractive man, very boyish, and at the end of lunch he galloped out of the house to go and play tennis.

In the car, when my father asked if I had liked Calvin—that was his name, obviously—I said yes. When my father asked what I thought of Calvin's work, I laughed. "That man never worked!" I said. But it turned out that Calvin did work, that he was a writer named Calvin Tomkins, that I had even been a fan of his for years. In England I had even worked with him on the telephone, editing a piece on Buckminster Fuller for *Queen*. It was a measure of his upper-class reticence that in five hours of conversation he had never told me his last name.

I taught Calvin how to love me after that. At night, before he went back to the suburbs, we met at a bar close to my office. I drank bullshots, because I knew I would be at work all night. At *Newsweek* everyone worked late and almost everyone drank. The magazine was structured with layers of editors, reporters, and writers so that if one writer turned in an incoherent piece, there was always someone else, someone who happened to be sober that day, to rewrite it into coherent *Newsweek* style.

Soon Calvin and I were leaving our offices—his at a magazine on Forty-fourth Street, mine on Forty-ninth Street—and having lunches in out-of-the-way French restaurants in midtown; the kind of places filled with matinee women and trysting couples. Within a few weeks we were having lunch together every day and spending afternoons at my apartment in bed. I taught him how to lie to his wife; he was always amazed that she believed him. I taught him how to cheat. If Warren was the dark side of my need for men, Calvin was the light side. Within six months he had left his chic wife and was living in a rented studio on Ninety-fifth Street.

Calvin said he thought Warren was treating me dreadfully; he said he would treat me as wonderfully as I deserved to be treated. I had lobbied for a transfer to *Newsweek*'s San Francisco offices. When I got the transfer, I couldn't get Warren on the telephone. "You know what I think," Calvin said. I told the editors of *Newsweek* that I didn't want to go to San Francisco after all. When I finally got Warren on the phone two days later, I told him that I wasn't coming.

I told my father that I was in love with Warren but that I couldn't imagine making a life with him. I could imagine, I said, making a life with Calvin. "I worried that you and Warren were very uneven," my father said. It was 1976, and my father had been sober almost a year. He went to AA meetings almost every day. When I met him for lunch in New York City, he always got to the restaurant on time—we ate at the Algonquin or at the Four Seasons. I was always late, and by the time I got there he was drinking his iced tea. My white wine—ordered by him—was waiting for me on the table. He knew how important it was for someone like me to have a drink waiting for them. That's the kind of thing alcoholics understand about other alcoholics, but my father never talked to me about my drinking; not then, not ever. I wonder though how it must have felt for him to order me that drink.

One of the things I loved about married men, aside from the intensity with which they loved you, an intensity compounded of attraction and the relief of escaping from their lives, was that, as the mistress of a married man, I had a lot of time to myself and almost unlimited freedom. During the months I was passionately involved with both Warren and Calvin, months during which they were both hard at work deconstructing the lives they had built for themselves, I had plenty of time to shop, read, work, gossip, and have long lunches with other men. I also spent a lot of time at my parents' house in Ossining.

When my father went to his nightly AA meeting, he sometimes took me along for companionship. I never dreamed that I had anything to learn from an organization like Alcoholics Anonymous. I remembered when my father first tried AA in the late sixties. His story was that he went to a meeting and someone said, "Hey! There's John Cheever!" so he didn't go back for ten years. I didn't blame him.

The first meeting he took me to was in the parish house of the Presbyterian Church on Route 9, right across the street from the little house behind the wall of Beechwood. A group of ordinary-looking suburban adults sat around a long refectory table. One told a story; it was a story about being young and rich and going to Yale and drinking too much. When it got to the point where the young man—now a middle-aged banker from Chappaqua—was arrested for drunk driving, I emotionally stepped away. I had never been arrested for drunk driving. I loved the meeting, though. I loved hearing men talk about their feelings, about their anxieties for their children, about their irritation with their wives. I loved the stories I heard about hiding bottles, and about the ways people disguised their drinking while leading apparently normal lives as bankers or teachers or housewives.

At other meetings, I listened as men and women read from *Alcoholics Anonymous.* There were lots of suggestions in the book, and other stories about alcoholics. Sometimes the stories sounded like my story, but there was always some detail that was too bizarre to fit into my life. There was always something in every story that allowed me to keep my distance from the idea that I might be an alcoholic. I thought that to be an alcoholic, a person had to be in terrible trouble. I was fine, I thought. I thought alcoholics were people who had heart attacks and delirium tremens the way my father did. I thought that alcoholics were told again and again by their friends and doctors that they should stop drinking. No one had ever said much about my drinking.

Two white window shades were unrolled on the wall at each meeting, with the twelve steps and twelve traditions of Alcoholics Anonymous printed on them. While the voices droned on around the table, I read the first few steps. We admitted we are powerless over alcohol—that our lives had become unmanageable. I was a thirty-year-old woman with a high-profile, dead-end job and no real prospects. I was writing copy about swimsuit fashions for a magazine that had never had a woman at the top editorial level. I cared about nothing. I was involved with two married men. I had nothing better to do than hang around my parents' house on weekends. But when I saw that word, *unmanageable,* I immediately thought about other people I knew and how their lives were definitely out of control.

In AA meetings I heard people talk as if their feelings were something they were responsible for. I heard grown-ups talk who didn't blame other people for their anxieties and irritations. I had never heard anyone talk that way. If I was angry at Calvin because he flirted with another woman, wasn't that his fault? If I panicked because he decided he needed to spend a weekend with his wife to be sure that their marriage was over, wasn't that because of something he had done wrong? I didn't understand how the way other people's behavior upset me could be changed by changing the way I reacted. I thought *they* had to change. I purposefully went about changing them.

At the same time, I saw how much my father had changed since he stopped drinking. He seemed to notice the rest of us for the first time. More impressive, he seemed to notice that the world worked in a certain way, that the house wasn't cleaned by gremlins, that dishes weren't just magically washed, that someone had to cook dinner for it to be served. He seemed to realize for the first time that driving out from New York in a bad rainstorm might be a chore.

At another meeting, in Croton, where we all sat in rows on folding chairs, I heard a woman talk about being married to an alcoholic. The man sounded a lot like Robert. She said her own drinking had been covered up by her husband's. I congratulated myself on leaving Robert, and for the first time I wondered if *he* was an alcoholic. And of course I drank right along with him. Then the woman talked about hiding bottles. I never hid bottles.

At first, as part of teaching Calvin to cheat, I urged him to cheat on me. He needed to break loose, I told him, not just from the confines of his marriage, but from the confines of any kind of monogamous relationship. At one of our lunches one day—I forget if it was at La Grillade or Le Moal—he told me that he had, in fact, been cheating on me. He had lied to me twice about going to the movies by himself and going home alone when, in fact, he had been sleeping with another woman. He expected that I would be pleased. Instead, I was devastated. "He should have known that you didn't mean it," my father said as we drove to the Bedford AA meeting. I sat in the room and seethed while a man told his story. He drank, he forgot things, his life kept falling apart in ways he didn't understand. When he drank, terrible things happened; people betrayed him.

I lived alone in those days, in an apartment at the top of an old brick building with marble lintels on Seventy-fourth Street at Lexington Avenue. My windows and a door opened out to a tar-paper roof surrounded by a nine-foot-high wall punctuated with semicircular turrets. In the back, the turrets were brick, but looking up from the street I could see that they were marble lion's heads. It was a romantic apartment. I remember Robert, teetering on the parapet, threatening to throw himself off the roof during a fight. There was a bottle of wine at the foot of the parapet. As I remember that night, as I remember watching his awkward, lanky form framed against the sky, I remember that I was laughing at him. With Robert gone, I felt I had put all that unhappiness behind me.

Calvin left his wife and went back to her and left her again. I wondered about my decision not to go to San Francisco. My misery at *Newsweek* got worse. Calvin thought I should quit. He thought I should try to write. He thought we should go off and live somewhere so that I could write and he could write his book. I like to say that I ran off to the south of France with someone else's husband. That makes it sound like another glamorous adventure; it wasn't another glamorous adventure. It was the beginning of a new life—again.

Tais-Toi

*C*alvin and I left for France in June, and we came home in
March, ten months later, changed forever. We flew to Paris
and drove south, lugging our bags into a dreary house with a
misleading name—Les Amandiers—on a ridge above a small,
undistinguished French village, Fayence. Back in New York,
when we rented the house from a down-at-the-heels English-
woman we had met through a friend of a friend, Les Amandiers had conjured up visions of flowering almond trees and
graceful arches. Our landlady called it "my villa."

In the distance, from Les Amandiers' kitchen, decorated with
stick-on linoleum tile, we could see the Estérel, the mountains
between us and the sea. In the morning we woke up and made
strong French coffee and separated to work. At first I worked
downstairs at a nicked old desk pushed against the wall with a
patio at my back. I wasn't sure what to write. I took out my old
journals from San Francisco and began using scenes from my

time there and free-associating. Most of the time I just typed away without thinking. Story after story floated to the surface of my mind. The prose seemed to burn right on the page. I reread each page over and over again, amazed at how stirring the words seemed to me. When I got to a stopping place I would wander outside into the sun and watch the ants making nests in the sandy earth around the house.

Then we had lunch—tomatoes, basil, the local oil, bread, and a couple of bottles of wine—and then we took a nap. We bought wine in huge five-gallon jugs that were filled from a re-fitted gas pump in the sheds of the local vineyard. There was a pump for red and a pump for white. At home we funneled the jug wine into bottles. The marc, a strong liqueur made from the leavings in the bottoms of the barrels, was a favorite of ours. The sheds were filled with all the wonderful things made from grapes, from pears and from plums. In the dark shelves at the back, the vintners stacked bottles of Mirabelle and Poire, with their rough tastes and the raw feelings they left in your mouth and the way they filled your brain like liquid heat.

In the afternoons I kept a journal and wrote letters and worked on my tan, lying on our tiny terrace, my body covered with oil. My mother came to visit us, my brother Fred came; sometimes people dropped in for lunch, sometimes we drove south to a dinner party, but our days had a monotony to them that gave my fictional world a chance to grow and thrive. By October I had written a novel.

In fact I wasn't even sure it was a novel. It seemed too short to me. I counted and recounted the words in the English books I had, to see if my book was long enough. I asked my mother. "Are you sure it's not just a short story?" she wrote back, confirming my doubts. Even if I had written a novel, I had nowhere to send it. I wrote to the husband of a friend who was also an agent, asking if he would read it. Then I took it to the post office. The French are a thrifty people, and the postmaster insisted that I send the manuscript book rate. It took three weeks to get to New York.

One day, at Cannes, strolling on the *croisette*—the sidewalk along the beach—we ran into Julia Child. Calvin had written a profile of her. We were instantly drawn into Julia's world; she exerted a tremendous magnetic force and commanded us to come for dinner at her little house in Plascassier. Over dinner, a chicken rouille with eggplant caviar and a rich chocolate dessert, Julia insisted that we abandon the cinder block and linoleum of Les Amandiers and live in her house. Winter was coming. She and her husband, Paul, were going back to Cambridge for the season. We would be too cold over there in the Var. Calvin and I eyed the cozy house with its heat registers and telephone—telephone!—and said certainly.

At Thanksgiving we ate crevettes and drank Baumes de Venise for dessert on a terrace above the sea at a restaurant in Cannes near the casino. Then we loaded the secondhand Simca we had bought from our local mechanic and headed back toward Cannes to La Pitchoune, the little house Julia and Paul had built on the estate of Julia's friend and collaborator Simone Beck. It was a simple, single-level stucco-and-tile house on a terrace, which Julia and Paul had built before Julia became a television star. There was a small living room with French doors leading out to a slate terrace, a hall with two bedrooms off it, and, at the back, the kitchen.

Julia's kitchen had nothing sentimental or romantic about it. There were no gingham curtains or French tiles or little pots of herbs or wooden tables. It was as businesslike as a garage. A long wooden island stood at the middle, with wooden counters on every side. All the wall space was covered with Peg-Board, decorated with the outlines of the dozens of kitchen tools that were hung there—everything from a set of wire whisks to basters to slotted spoons. Calvin and I took turns cooking there. We found the dishes under the counters, and we had fun cooking Julia's recipes in Julia's kitchen and serving them on Julia's plates—looking just the way they looked in her big picture books.

We hadn't been there long when the phone rang one night after dinner. It was Peter Matson, the agent I had sent my novel to. Three editors wanted to buy it, he told me. He was asking $25,000 and was sure he'd get it. I thanked Peter and hung up, but the world suddenly started to sway underneath me. I didn't know what to do. Nothing I had done had ever come to fruition before. I felt sick.

We got in the Simca and drove down to Cannes, but it was late, restaurants were closing and the casino was shut. It didn't matter, there was no way to celebrate this unthinkable success. I shivered in the cold wind of the *croisette*. Cannes looked sinister to me that night. There were women in short fur coats and tight skirts soliciting outside the Carlton Hotel. We drove home. I opened a bottle of whiskey and two cans of beans I had found in Julia's cabinets. Calvin went to bed. I drank and stared at the fire until I saw that morning was coming. The whiskey was gone. The next day was even stranger. I felt as if I had been shot out of a cannon—as if I had no skin and my nerves were hanging out exposed. We played tennis, and I lost. When I was overwhelmed by my feelings, I poured a glass of calvados or sherry into the bubbly translucent blue of Julia's glasses from Biot. I was a disaster waiting to happen.

I knew perfectly well, though, that I had hardly anything to do with my own success. It was like the writing itself. In the morning I would sit down at the typewriter and begin a scene. I would decide where to start. Often when I began, another scene emerged, or a character I hadn't even thought about. The characters I had invented seemed to be increasingly out of control. I was amazed at their antics—far more outrageous and odd than anything I had planned for them. My typing became like the scything in the famous scene in *Anna Karenina* when Levin learns to scythe with the farmers. After many starts, he picks up a rhythm of scything; a rhythm that lets him scythe row after row in a kind of trance. When he loses the rhythm it's almost impossible to get down one row. When he has the rhythm the rows are done almost effortlessly, although he's sweating and his muscles ache. I always thought that scything scene was somehow about prayer.

As I've become a more accomplished writer with each book, I have relinquished more control over my writing. It's true I have to sit down and spend the time writing, but beyond that, what happens doesn't seem to be up to me. I used to think that to write I had to have six uninterrupted hours of quiet. Since then I have written well in all sorts of circumstances: with a baby playing in the crib next to me, late at night or at dawn when the household is asleep. It no longer surprises me that Shirley Jackson wrote her best story on the way home from the market on an overcast day in North Bennington, Vermont, with two children in a stroller. I have also written badly in all sorts of circumstances: in a room alone with all the time in the world; in a study at Yaddo, with the lawns rolling away in the distance and the memory of Robert Penn Warren's previous occupancy of that same room. In the end I believe that if a book wants to be written, it will get written—wherever the writer happens to be. If a book doesn't want to get written, there will be hell to pay.

Near the end of our time at Julia's La Pitchoune, Calvin began working at a nearby house in the mornings. My nerve endings were so raw that I was unable to work if I could hear him working in his room down the hall. One morning, just as I was finishing a volume of Anthony Powell's series of novels *A Dance to the Music of Time,* I heard some strange noises around the house. I was engrossed in the novel and lay in bed until I had finished it. Then I felt sluggish because I was still in bed. I thought about just rolling over and going back to sleep. I thought about going into the kitchen, pouring a brandy, and then going back to bed. Then I heard more noises. I imagined it was Julia's cat, Grisaille, scratching to get in, but when I went to the door she wasn't there.

I went to the bathroom and took a shower in the tub. Over the sound of the water, I thought there were other noises. I told myself it was the mistral, the French winter wind, which had been blowing for days, turning the leaves of the poplars over and flattening the mimosa against the rich Provençal earth. I wrapped a towel around myself and went down the hall to my bedroom. A man was standing there. He was a short, stocky man in a green flak jacket, and he stared at me, blankly. I was too surprised to understand what was happening. At first I thought he must be a gardener or a plumber. "*Puis-je vous aider?*" I said.

"*Tais-toi,*" he said ferociously. Shut up. Then I knew he wasn't the gardener. "This is it," were the words that formed in my head. I felt as if I had been waiting for this, this terror. I stepped backwards, trying to back out of the room, clutching the towel around me. I began to scream in a voice that sounded as if it were coming from outside me. The man came toward me, backing me up against the rough stucco wall of the living room. I saw the olive trees out the window. I grabbed for a brass standing lamp. Then he hit me, hard enough so that I heard a crack and blacked out. When I came to a few seconds later I was on the floor with the lamp lying beside me. I scrambled to my feet but the man was gone. I fumbled with one of the doors, got it open, and saw him fleeing away over the terraces between the olive groves.

Still wrapped in the towel, I ran next door to the Becks'. The police came in their big Citroëns with their sirens blaring. During the course of the afternoon they produced two evil-looking men in green flak jackets; I didn't recognize them. Later that evening, Calvin and I went down to Cannes and bought a pistol. After that, every afternoon, instead of playing tennis, I went out to the local dump and practiced shooting. I willed the man in the flak jacket to come back so that I could kill him.

I thought he would come back for me. At night I closed the big shutters. One night I wandered into the kitchen to pour myself a glass of marc. There were no shutters in the kitchen; I was sure he was out there watching me. There was a scratch at the window, and I screamed again and again. I was sure it was him. I could hear my own screams reverberating around the kitchen and into the hallway. Calvin leapt out of bed and stumbled and went sprawling on the hall floor. I was still screaming. Later I realized the scratching had been Grisaille the cat trying to get in. Grisaille never came back. After we left, Julia wrote us to say she had disappeared.

In the afternoons, while Calvin was working, I sometimes drove the Simca north into the hill towns, over toward the Gorges du Loup, or down the coast toward Italy. It was always raining. I was always afraid. And somewhere deep below the surface of my conscious mind I was beginning to make a connection between drinking and the bad things that happened to me when I was drinking. The problem wasn't that I was often drunk; the problem was that I was a drunk.

One afternoon I drove to Vence to see the chapel where Matisse had covered the walls with the silhouettes of the saints. I thought it would be something like the rose window at the church in Pocantico Hills, where Matisse filled a circle with bright pink and green glass like an explosion of sweetness. The chapel was black and white, stark, and I could see the rain falling outside. If you had asked me then if I believed in God, I would have said yes. The truth was that I didn't know what that meant. My faith was a great whiteness like the walls of that chapel, with occasional fault lines of belief.

I didn't understand that faith could provide me with a way to live my life—that, in fact, was the point. I had no way to process the things that happened to me that year—whether it was having my novel published or the free fall into fear that began after my encounter with the man in the flak jacket. I had no idea how to respond to good things; eating a can of beans and drinking a bottle of whiskey was the best I could do; or how to respond to bad things; buying a pistol and spending afternoons at the dump blasting the empty cans was the best I could do.

We left France a few weeks later and moved back into my apartment on Seventy-fourth Street. Before, when I had lived there alone, I was immune to the fears of a single woman in the city. My apartment was on the roof, I boasted. To break in, someone would have to land in a helicopter. When people talked about being mugged or held up, I immediately distanced myself from them, finding something different in our experiences—they were older or younger; they lived in a worse neighborhood; they lived in Chicago—that allowed me to believe that what had happened to them couldn't happen to me. Now it had happened to me, and I was afraid. Living on the roof suddenly terrified me. Anyone who wanted could just come up the building's back stairs, or up the fire escape, or even up in the elevator; they could climb the rickety iron stairs to the roof and jump down onto my terrace. I had sent my pistol to myself at my New York address, and when Calvin wasn't there, I took to sleeping with it next to the bed.

On the outside, though, all was triumphant. I called my novel *Looking for Work*. Warner Brothers optioned the movie rights for more than the publisher had paid as an advance against royalties. Calvin and I went to Arizona to see his daughter, and then we drove to Los Angeles, stopping at the Grand Canyon and the Hopi mesas. In Los Angeles we had dinner with Joan Didion and John Dunne, and they said that they had heard that my book was going to be a hit. A few weeks before it was published in January of 1980, my father took me out to lunch. "I'm worried that I never prepared you for success," he said over the oyster stew in the Oyster Bar. Later, driving to the country for a weekend, Calvin had to pull the car over. I knelt on the gravel shoulder of the Hutchinson River Parkway and retched.

That winter we were in California again, and I called Warren. I hadn't spoken to him for five years. I thought of him often, thought of him as the only man I had ever really loved. Whatever happened, I imagined, there was a sadness at the core of my heart. Our love, I still believed, was a great love, even if it was a great love that could never be. Calvin had to go up to San Francisco, and I went too. I met Warren for lunch. "How come you got so thin?" he said.

Warren knows San Francisco so well that it's like being in his own house to be there with him. He took me to a bar with wooden booths. We ate delicious chowder and drank white wine. He drank vodka and grapefruit; it was lunchtime, but I could see he had just gotten up. I wondered who he had been in bed with. I drank more white wine. "Let's get you a real drink," he said, and he signaled the bartender and ordered a glass of Famous Grouse, my favorite scotch—a double. I felt completely at home with Warren, as if my psyche had just been waiting to find him again so that it could hum and relax. Then he drove me up to the top of Twin Peaks. The city spread out before us, below the gigantic hood of Warren's 1975 Chevy Impala. "I still love you," he said, and he kissed me. I was late for dinner with Calvin.

Later that spring, Warren came to New York. I met him in someone else's apartment where he had holed up to write about the Irish Republican Army. He had just come back from months in Belfast. I wore my new Perry Ellis white linen pants with a halter and strappy white sandals; I brought us a picnic lunch from Eli Zabar. Warren answered the door in a terrorist's knitted mask and with a towel wrapped around him. He was holding a bottle of whiskey. In the end, leaving him, I felt as if I was escaping something intense. It was like walking out of a hothouse into the real world. I was relieved to get back to my prim little life with my good clothes and the parties where Calvin and I were part of a predictable world of intelligent art collectors and writers. I didn't see Warren again for another five years.

Sometime that summer I decided that I wanted to have a baby. I had always claimed that the last thing I wanted to do was have a baby. Was it the same instinct that caused me to vow I would never be a writer? A kind of fear of saying what I really, desperately wanted out loud so that if I didn't get it I could pretend I never wanted it? I don't even know. When I said that I thought it would be fun to have a kid, Calvin blanched. He had three children. He was almost sixty years old. By then we had made each other quite unhappy. I had left him because he was so slow getting divorced. Then I had come back; then I left again. Now I wanted a child. In the meantime, I developed a series of crushes on other men. I was a dangerous, pretty thirty-nine-year-old in expensive clothes.

TWENTY-THREE

Champagne

The most important decisions I made—to leave *Newsweek*, to have a child—seemed to be made outside me somehow. Really, I wanted to have a child just because I didn't want to miss having a child. In another way, I just floated forward through my own life's story with what seems like, in retrospect, very little control. In fact the less control I had, the better my life got. Even then it felt as if I were part of someone else's plan. This was the rhythm of my drinking. There was no drama in the drinking itself; there were no convulsions or car accidents or people saying that I was "hitting the bottle" or "headed for skid row." Instead there was just a slow deterioration of my sanity, my judgment, and the odd way that so much of what I did added up to nothing. All the drama was in the life.

One of these dramas was the future of my affair with Calvin. We had been together for three years, when I decided I wanted to have a child. He did not want a child. The drama played itself out in one of my favorite venues, the Ritz Hotel in Boston. I loved its grand rooms and its sweeping views over the Boston Common. Calvin and I made love, but when I tried to get him to talk, he didn't want to talk. I could almost feel him slipping away from me. I went to have lunch with a friend. It was hard to eat, even the white wine didn't help. I felt as if he had called my bluff. I was losing him. Then when I was packed and it was time to go to the airport, something happened. We were going through the revolving door, out onto Newbury Street. That's when great moments happen: midway through the revolving door, or in the back of a cab, or walking against the traffic up Madison, or in the airport lounge waiting for someone to get on a plane. "I don't want to lose you," he said. He didn't know that I was desperately thinking the same thing. We talked and talked, and when I went back to New York I had what I wanted.

So I stopped using birth control. I had never been pregnant, never had an abortion, although I felt that I had taken plenty of chances with my slippery diaphragm and my impossible-to-remember birth control pills. I didn't think about it much. I went on working, and Calvin moved us into a floor-through apartment on Eighty-first Street. At the end of July, on my birthday, we drove out to Southampton and spent the weekend walking on the beach and lounging in a motel. We felt as if we needed a rest—but from what?

At my birthday dinner we drank a few bottles of champagne. I drank buckets of champagne in those days: it replaced beer as the staple of my diet. If Warren was a beer and whiskey man, Calvin was a champagne type. We ordered it by the case, Domaine de Chandon or Krug, and we drank it without thinking about glasses or even bottles. When we sat down to chat or read, we drank champagne. Often we went through a case in a day or two. Looking back, I guess I had a champagne buzz on for two or three years.

I remember my first book party. We were friends with Brooke Hayward and Peter Duchin, and Janet Maslin was my best friend. I had met Janet at *Newsweek.* Night after night I went back with her to her ground-level apartment and complained about my life with all its drama—the married boyfriends, the unmarried boyfriends. Later Janet married my brother Ben, and they have been married for fifteen years. Janet and Brooke and my editor Nan Talese gave me a lunch at Elaine's. I was very nervous. My parents were very nervous. The party was fine, but afterwards we went back to my apartment. We chatted and killed a few bottles of champagne. Somehow I needed all that to take the edge off, and I loved Calvin for keeping me company. I didn't really think of champagne as something I drank, I thought of it as liquid, fizzy glamour, something that just went with having famous, rich friends—although none of us were ever famous enough or rich enough—and having book parties at Elaine's.

I'm sitting at my desk in Yaddo, and a light snow is falling. My daughter, Sarah, is fifteen now. On the way up here, in a rented car, I drove fast and noticed a few speed traps. I've been coming to Yaddo for a decade to work on my writing in the same place that Carson McCullers and Katherine Anne Porter and my father worked on theirs. I love the writers' colony atmosphere, the long silences, the time to brood. I'm always in a hurry as I go north. In Newburgh a cop with a radar gun was standing on the lane divider and pointing the gun at the passing flow of cars; half a mile later, two cars were flashing their lights and pulling cars over. I was speeding through Coxsackie in a daze, daydreaming about a time ten years before, the time Warren and I drove up to Yaddo together and we got here just at dusk on a spring evening and I let us into the Mansion and we were alone there and I was in Katrina's bedroom and he sat in Foster's study with the evening light coming in through the stained-glass windows and wrote his column. Yaddo was magical then; Warren was magical then. Yaddo is still magical.

On the way up, Warren and I had stopped in Coxsackie, and we went into a local bar. After I had a few beers with him and he had settled down with the local papers—Warren loved newspapers almost as much as he loved the bars he read them in and the drinks he drank while he was reading them—I went to an antiques store and bought a brass mirror I couldn't afford, and I thought, well, maybe we'll settle down in a nice place like Coxsackie and Sarah will play in the country and she will have her own pony.

As I passed the Coxsackie exit this time, there were two state trooper cars on the shoulder flashing their lights, and one of the troopers stuck his arm out the window of the driver's side and beckoned me over. I wasn't even scared. I didn't argue with him. In fact, I had been speeding. He came around to the passenger side of the car, because there were cars whizzing by on the driver's side, and rapped on the window. I lowered it.

"Let me see your license and registration, I mean license and rental agreement," he said. "Have you been drinking?"

"No," I said. I gave him my license and rental agreement.

"Are you sure?" he said. "You didn't have a little something with lunch?" And I thought about all the years when I never drove without a can of beer in my lap and a six-pack of beer in the car, and all the years when there was a bowl of ice on the floor on the passenger side to keep the beer cool, and all the times I passed a bottle back and forth while I was driving. And I said, "No, officer, no. I haven't had a drink in five years."

TWENTY-FOUR

"I really want a drink."

That summer Calvin and I were living in an apartment on Eighty-first Street, my father had a kidney operation. He was dying, but we didn't know it yet. I was pregnant, but I didn't know it yet. My father had been sober for five years. In July, Calvin and I decided to go to France the way we sometimes did in the summer. I didn't want to just drive around though, so I decided that we should backpack down the Loire from town to town. That way we would get exercise and stay thin. It was very important to stay thin. We would walk through the vineyards of the Loire. We would see France in a different way.

We flew to Paris and checked into the Ritz and went to Le Vieux Campeur for our sleeping bags and backpacks. The Ritz doorman didn't want to let us in when we got back—he thought we were backpackers. I thought this was very funny. We had a tiny room, dripping with molding that was all painted in six different shades of gray, and it had a wrought-iron balcony outside the French windows. Later I painted every New York apartment I had in four or five shades of gray with indifferent effect.

We took the train to Orléans and began our hike. French hiking books show every turn of every trail, and we headed down the north bank of the Loire on a narrow dirt path. It was hot. We ran out of water. We ran out of wine. We stopped for lunch on a grassy hill above the river, but by the late afternoon we were exhausted and thirsty. Horses galloped by us on the dike along the trail. That night we set up our tent at the edge of a French campground where French families had tents in the shape of houses, complete with imprinted curtains and geraniums in window boxes. We finished the bottle of bourbon we had brought for the hike. We had walked too far. We sat under the trees in a strange country. We walked into the nearest town and had a big meal and some wine. That made me feel much better, but by the next morning I was exhausted again.

We got as far down the river as Tours, after a night in which the wind blew our tent so hard I couldn't sleep. Stomach cramps hit me so hard in the Vieux Carré of Tours, as we walked along the ancient streets, that I had to sit down on the fourteenth-century curb until they passed. At night we drank wine and champagne, in the morning we spiked our coffee with calvados. The next morning we rented a car and drove to the fanciest château hotel in the area. They put us—we were backpackers after all—in an attic room.

We put on our bathing suits and walked out to the swimming pool. The night before we had slept on the ground. In the pool was a blond American girl. A German man perfected his tan while a brace of Doberman pinschers looked on. We spread out uncomfortably in the sun—I noticed that my arms and legs were pale where my hiking shorts had been and that tiny spider veins were appearing on my skin. From behind the cabana walked John Gregory Dunne and Joan Didion. "Susan?" John said.

That night we had dinner with the Dunnes and Jane Kramer, who, as it turned out, lived nearby. I couldn't shake the feeling of disorientation I had from the hike. I sipped a glass of wine, and it felt like liquid lead. Later, in Paris, I was sick at the Crazy Horse, I was sick at the Deux Magots, I was sick in the penthouse at the Montalambert. It wasn't until we got home that I realized I was pregnant.

There was a moment when I officially learned that I was pregnant—I was on the phone with Doctor Buchman's nurse, and she told me the results were positive. I was sitting in the narrow room where I worked in the apartment on Eighty-first Street, and I was suffused with this incredible joy. The walls seemed to be singing with it. Soon enough, pregnancy made me nauseous and cranky. I knew we would have to move. I knew I would gain weight. I knew I would have to stop drinking. I knew we would have to get married. We decided on a family ceremony at my parents', performed by a local justice of the peace. When it was over we let a dozen balloons fly into the sky over my parents' lawn. We spent our honeymoon night at a tiny hotel in North Salem. There were rose petals on the bed, and champagne and chocolate, and the whole thing seemed artificial and silly.

I had stopped drinking before. One of the reasons that I

knew I was not an alcoholic was that I could stop drinking. I had stopped drinking when I went to Weight Watchers a year earlier and lost forty pounds. After a few months on Weight Watchers, I began substituting a glass of wine for a fruit. Soon I gave up fruit altogether and drank wine instead. Occasionally I substituted a real drink—a martini or a scotch—for a serving of milk. It worked very well. Another problem when I stopped drinking though, was that my friends suddenly seemed very boring to me. Parties became interminable. I couldn't wait for dinner to be served and then for dinner to be over. I went from being someone who never wanted to go home to being someone who couldn't wait to get home.

I realized that people often repeated themselves and often told the same story over and over again. I had no tolerance for this. One night I remember being at Marie Winn's house with the people I admired the most—Janet Malcolm and Gardner Botsford and the Angells: these were the people whose acquaintance I treasured. They started telling the story about Lillian Ross's dog Goldie. Everyone knew that Mr. Shawn, who was then the editor of *The New Yorker,* was having a long-term affair with Lillian Ross even though he always went out in public with his wife, Cecile. First Roger Angell told everyone how he had been in Mr. Shawn's office one day and Lillian Ross's little dog Goldie had trotted in. Goldie had leapt into his lap as Mr. Shawn protested that he had no idea why Goldie was so friendly to him. "Down, Goldie, Down," Roger mimicked in an imitation of Mr. Shawn's infinitely quiet voice. Everyone laughed. Then about forty-five minutes later, Gardner told the same story. Everyone laughed even harder. I don't know if my friends were drinking too much. The fact that they were drinking at all when I wasn't drove me nuts. I felt crazier when I wasn't drinking than when I was drinking. By the time Calvin got around to telling the story, I wasn't laughing anymore. Soon I just stopped going to parties.

At the beginning of December, when I was pregnant enough to be in maternity clothes, we flew out to California to see Calvin's first grandchild, and while we were there my father called me. He told me that he and my mother had been to the doctor that day. I was sitting in a hotel room in La Jolla, wearing a maternity sweater. My mother got on the other phone. My father said the doctor said that he had cancer and that the cancer had gone to his bones. He had called my brother Fred, he said, and Fred had said he would come home to visit. "Some parents will do anything to get their kids to come home for Christmas," my father cracked. It wasn't really funny.

We flew out of La Jolla and back to New York, and I drove to Ossining the next day. My father was lying in the bed in my old bedroom. He looked dead already. We took him to Memorial Sloan-Kettering Hospital in New York. The doctors talked a lot of mumbo jumbo about percentages and protocols, and even if they had been telling the truth we wouldn't have been able to understand them. My father embarked on an excruciatingly painful series of protocols of radiation and chemotherapy. I would go to Memorial and talk to him and visit him. I remember one afternoon when I was wheeling him to a radiation appointment, he turned around and looked at me; he was bald by then, and his blue eyes seemed huge in his shrunken face. The walls on either side of him were pale green and decorated with prints of spring flowers. "You know," he said, "I really want a drink sometimes." I didn't know what to say. "I understand, Daddy," I said. My father had been sober for seven years when he died.

Even in the days before I gave birth, I wasn't sure if I really wanted a baby. I didn't tell Calvin that; he had paid too much for my decision. We had bought a co-op and moved in. His retirement money and my father's money had all been sunk into the apartment—and it wasn't a very grand apartment. A few weeks before I was due, I visited my friend Susan, who had already had her baby. Susan looked beautiful, but the baby was clearly a major pain in the ass. Susan had been transformed somehow, I could see that, but when the baby cried, I winced. When Susan laid the baby down on its back to change its diaper, the smell made me feel sick. I was nine months pregnant. I promised myself I would never have to change my baby—I would hire someone to do it.

I went to the hospital reluctantly. In the end I had a C-section. The epidural hurt, and the C-section was strangely violent. I could feel this great wrenching and pulling and yanking, but there was no pain. Finally, Dr. Buchman pulled out the baby, a baby girl, my baby girl. I held her for a moment, and my life changed. I wept when they took her away to clean her.

The feelings I had then were more powerful than anything I had ever felt, and they were instantaneous. They transcended the pain and sweetness of my life before that moment, and they soared above the exhilaration of the perfect flute of champagne or the comfort of a martini shimmering in its glass at the end of a long, dry day. I knew I had something to live for, and I was as surprised as anyone. Suddenly someone else existed; someone else's welfare was more important than my own. In the instant of Sarah's birth, I got the gift of being able to love.

Sarah

*E*arly in my life I learned to gauge others' moods and to guess what they were thinking. This is certainly a characteristic of children who grow up in alcoholic households, but I'm sure I would have done it anyway. I want to hold the whole world in my mind. In all my love affairs and friendships this is a problem—since I know what you are thinking and feeling, I can respond to it and limn your response and so on. I can get pretty tangled up this way, and you can end up feeling pretty unimportant. Until the moment when Sarah was born I don't believe another person had really penetrated that dense web of protecting reactions and judgments I had used to get along in the world.

I remember holding Sarah and feeling some force outside me literally infuse me with confidence. That flash of feeling I had when the nurse told me I was pregnant came back. Day after day as I held her, I could feel myself changing.

Early every morning my father would call—in the hospital, I was always up, and he was an early riser, especially after he got sick. He could feel what was happening to me; it was so powerful he thought it was happening to him too. "I've kicked it," he said. "I'm getting better!" He thought the cancer was gone. He knew the vibrations of the love I was feeling for my baby were reaching him out there in Ossining. Two months later he was dead.

I was a different person though. The woman who found out that her father was going to die and took to her bed in La Jolla, the woman who felt as if her father's illness was something that was happening to her, was beginning to disintegrate and dry up and blow away in this scorching, powerful wind of love. I had always worried about dropping my baby—before I had her. I remember holding Sarah and knowing I wouldn't drop her. I loved every bit of her tiny body. She was hardly bigger than a pile of books or a pet, but my whole soul focused on her—and that was how I discovered that I had a soul. I was amazed at my feelings. I would have been happy to die to protect Sarah, except that her need for me made me want to take care of myself in a new, practical way. There was a reason to live now; not just the joy, the soaring feelings, the suffusing warmth, but the reality of being needed. When she was an infant, Sarah had a little musical pillow that played "Here comes Peter Cottontail, hopping down the bunny trail." I told my friend Brooke that the music to Peter Cottontail had become my *Messiah*, my B minor Mass. Our friendship began to fray.

I couldn't bear to let Sarah cry. I attuned myself to her body so carefully that any physical need she had was met even be-

fore she could express it. Then, the day after I took her home
to the apartment on Central Park West, the doctor called. We
had chosen a Waspy pediatrician, a restrained sort of guy with
trellis wallpaper in his office. I would have to drop Sarah back
at the hospital, he said, she had jaundice. I took her to the hospital in the Snugli, the cotton front-pack she rode in. We
waited. Then when it was our turn, they laid her down on a
table and stuck needles into her. She screamed, and when I
tried to hold her, they held me back. Maybe it's necessary to
treat children this way in order to do tests on them; it broke
my heart. God knows what it did to Sarah. They said I should
go home, so I sat next to her incubator on a plastic chair. Finally someone took pity on me and showed me to a guest
room where Sarah and I could sleep. It cost a hundred dollars
a night. I called my father in tears. Don't worry, he said, don't
worry.

We were in Lenox Hill Hospital for three days that time.
Then a month later we were back. My little Sarah was often
sick. This time she had a slight tremor in her arms and legs.
Sarah had a week of tests, a week of torture. Slowly she got better for no apparent reason. After that we changed pediatri-
cians. Still, she had a urinary tract condition that required
painful tests, and she had serious pneumonia, twice. This time
we lived at Mount Sinai. I slept curled around her little body
on the hospital bed. The baby in the next room had AIDS—
but it was 1982 and I had never heard of AIDS. I had also never
heard that there was any connection between maternal drinking and a child's health.

Sarah doesn't remember the shrieking, the pain and the way her father and I stood by and wrung our hands and wept as doctors and nurses poked and prodded her, covered her with electrodes, sucked spinal fluid out of her tiny back. My children's early years are so vivid to me that it seems to me that their characters must have been formed before they even remember the light of day.

I alternated between panic at her fragileness, hope that she would someday grow into a little girl, and joy, just pure joy at her existence in the world. At night, when I walked her back and forth on our living room floor, the streetlights gave a strange striped feel to our apartment. With Sarah finally sleeping on my shoulder, I thought I was in heaven.

Sarah always woke up just before sunrise—she still does at age sixteen. Every morning I could hear her begin to murmur in her crib, and, looking out the window, I could see the sky begin to be stained pink, and then red flooding into the air from the east on the other side of Central Park, behind the monolith of Mount Sinai Hospital.

Many mornings, if it was warm enough, I loaded her into the backpack and walked her around the Upper West Side. The motion of the backpack and the closeness of our two bodies soothed both of us. I was exhausted, but I was whole. When Calvin and I traveled, we often loaded her into the backpack for an early morning walk so that her noise wouldn't wake the household. We walked with her along dirt roads in the Berkshires when we visited Gardner Botsford and Janet Malcolm, and we walked with her on the beach at Captiva when we visited Robert Rauschenberg. Sarah always went to sleep exactly at 7:30 at night. She was the perfect child for a New York couple. We continued to give dinner parties and even to go out for dinner after she was asleep. I loved falling asleep in my house, drunk from parties and drunk with pleasure, with my Sarah sleeping under my roof—even though my roof was the roof of an apartment building in the middle of Manhattan.

I hired a baby-sitter, but for the first year of Sarah's life I wouldn't let the baby-sitter take her out of the apartment. I was working in my old apartment on the other side of the park. I was writing about my father, spinning a web to keep him alive. In the morning I would leave Sarah—and leaving her felt like a knife in the heart—to go across the park and re-join my father and my past. After Sarah was born, I threw away the box of .22 longs that I had kept for my gun. I had some balance in my life, at last.

When I read my father's journals—a million words revealing his bisexuality, his depression, his struggles, his lack of focus on his children in general and me in particular—it was only coming home to Sarah that kept me from wallowing in bitterness. My family used to joke that the only straight thing about me was my hair. Who could grow up straight with a father like that?

Sarah did seem to be growing up straight. She was a brave little girl, a loving little girl. She was immensely proud of her own accomplishments, and her father and I were beside ourselves. We stopped drinking champagne—it seemed too frivolous for our new, serious station in life. We limited ourselves to evening drinks and good wine, lots of good wine. Raising a child is difficult, particularly in the late afternoon and evening when children are cranky and fussy. I took the edge off these hard hours with scotch and wine.

Calvin hadn't wanted another child, but he fell in love with his baby girl. One night when he was holding her in the rocking chair, she vomited on him and he didn't even move. He was the most fastidious man in the world, but he didn't care that vomit was all over his Brooks Brothers shirt and dripping down onto his flannels and his loafers. I loved him for loving her—and this was such a passion, such a consuming force, that after a while I wasn't sure if I loved him for himself at all anymore. I was still ruled by feelings. Like all alcoholics, I worshiped at the shrine of my own heart.

I Stop; I Start

They say that the children of alcoholics always marry alcoholics. If only it were that simple. An alcoholic family, like
any family, twists and turns and sometimes writhes and snaps
and howls. Children get certain ideas when growing up—usually from their parents—ideas about who they are and what
the world is like. These ideas are communicated in the time
before words, and they remain beyond words, if you ask me.
All the psychiatry and all the understanding and all the pars-
ing and poking and analyzing in the world doesn't seem to begin to describe an individual person. I didn't always marry
alcoholics at all. Robert may have been an alcoholic, but I
didn't know it—and neither did he.

Calvin certainly wasn't an alcoholic. He didn't have an ad-
dictive bone in his body. It never occurred to him that there
was anything good about having more or getting more. If he
had a drink, or something good to eat, that was enough for

him. It would never even occur to him to eat a pound of Brie or drink a bottle of wine. If I found something good, I always thought that more of it would be better.

Somehow though, Calvin had an idea about the world that went with my idea about the world. The simple thing would be to say that he needed alcoholism around him—that he was a co-dependent. The romantic thing would be to say that he fell in love with me. The true thing would be to say that all this is beyond human understanding, along with a lot of other things.

In 1984 we cashed in on the real estate boom and moved to a much more expensive apartment on the East Side. I had finished *Home Before Dark,* the book I wrote about my father. The move across town seemed like another new start, and I stopped drinking again—after Sarah was born I started going to a nutritionist, who prescribed exercise and sobriety. Our life began to get better. We seemed to have weathered the terrible year in which Sarah was born and my father died. In the spring of 1984, my brother Ben called to tell me that my mother had been diagnosed with cancer. It was hard to believe, I'll tell you. It felt as if lightning had struck twice in the same place—my heart. Once again I went to Memorial Sloan-Kettering on a parent's behalf. Once again I sat in the waiting room where I had spent hours with my father. I saw the baldness from chemotherapy and the wastedness from the disease and the drugs, and something inside me shut down and shifted. I had been told to take my mother's pathology slides to a Dr. O. When Dr. O. finally appeared, he was kind to me, and I began to fall in love with him.

The first afternoon we got together, he was with another woman. The three of us quickly locked ourselves into an emotional triangle that had nothing to do with each other and everything to do with—I think—ourselves. The woman's mother was also a patient of Dr. O. We all went out for dinner and drank a lot of red wine. The doctor loved the Hungarian restaurant where we ate; he loved the wine, which was called Bull's Blood. It was a special occasion. I began drinking again; after all, my mother was sick. What did anything matter? I began an affair with Dr. O.

I remember leaving Calvin riding Sarah around on the back of a bicycle in the driveway of a house we had rented in Bedford. The late afternoon sun was glistening on her downy little head. I was driving in to the city to go to a grimy apartment to sleep with a man I didn't even know. I couldn't help myself; I didn't see it. By the time my book about my father was published and my mother was better—after radiation treatments—Dr. O. was having an affair with the other woman. I returned to the wreckage of my marriage. These were years when I was drinking, but I don't even remember the drinking. I was acting as if I were a marionette being pulled around by the invisible strings that tied me to the past and my terrible needs and my dreadful expectations. How can I justify what I did then? Drinking doesn't absolve anyone of responsibility.

That winter I got involved with another man, Robert Massie, a writer who had been a friend of mine for a while, who lived in the suburbs. Bob Massie treated me with a seriousness that I craved. Reflected in his eyes, I saw myself as an important writer. "Does Calvin always marry beautiful women?" he asked me. One night I went to a party downtown and he drove in from the suburbs and picked me up and we went to my office and made love. Sarah and Calvin were asleep at home. For Calvin's sixtieth birthday, in 1985, I took us all to

Aspen. We skied Silver Bells and had a wonderful time. I loved skiing with Calvin. But all the time, as I pointed my skis downhill or as I worried about Sarah—who finally had a private instructor to take care of her—or as I threw my weight into a turn on the steep slope of North Star, I was thinking about Bob Massie. I was never there, but I was struggling to be there.

That summer I stopped drinking again. Sarah's new pediatrician suggested that I stop drinking. I didn't pause to wonder what made him suggest that. It wasn't hard to do, partly because my mind was so fuzzy and my memory so selective that I wasn't even aware that I *was* drinking. Calvin and Sarah and I had rented a house at the beach in Little Compton, Rhode Island. We had heard it was nice, so we had gone there. I remember one day when we were giving a dinner party and I went in the morning to buy the wine at the Sakonnet Vineyards. I tasted this and I tasted that and then I walked out into the sun, just vibrating with the fullness of it. I had started drinking and I didn't even know it. I thought of it as tasting.

I had no idea that the problems I had with men, with marriage, even with my work had anything to do with drinking. I had watched my father think the same thing. I had gone through the process of becoming—slowly, so slowly—aware that his problems and our family problems had something to do with his drinking. Even then, after all the AA meetings I had been to with my father, and after I had betrayed my husband and my beloved little girl over and over again, I still didn't see any connection between my drinking and my problems. I thought men were the problem. I thought Calvin and Bob and Dr. O. and Warren were the problem. I thought that drinking was a wonderful way I had of dealing with my problems. It worked. It even worked in dealing with Warren, who had begun commuting to New York to court me again after all those years. He had left his wife. He said we were still in love with each other. He said I needed to have another child. Sometimes, even though I was already intimately involved with Bob Massie and still living with Calvin, I slept with Warren in his hotel room. It's horrifying now, but it made perfect sense to me at the time. Afterwards we would have lunch. Warren made me feel safe. He knew everything about me, and it didn't horrify him: it didn't even seem to bother him.

There were a few months when I sometimes slept with three men in one day. I woke up with Calvin and took Sarah to school, or left her with a baby-sitter. I met Warren at his hotel room. I would always tell myself that I wasn't going to sleep with Warren; I always did. Being with him was like being in a bell jar. It would suck me in and take away my judgment. When I left him I would often find myself running, eager to get away and back to a life I understood. I could breathe again. In the afternoon, Bob would often meet me in my studio apartment. I didn't know that promiscuity can be a symptom of clinical depression. I only knew that I felt frantic all the time.

Something terrible happened when Warren and I combined, something terrible for both of us, and something so seductive and so compelling that neither of us could resist it. Warren's daughter Hilary came up from downtown where she was a student at NYU, and I took her out to lunch. "It's so sad," she told me. "You're the only woman Dad has ever really loved and you aren't together." I called Warren to tell him that I loved him too, but I couldn't get him on the phone.

The Sand at the Heart
of the Pearl

When I had Sarah, and when my father died, a lot of my old feelings started bumping around in the attic where I had put them. There were crashing sounds as if someone was going wild up there, and rattling sounds as if someone was trying to escape into my conscious mind. I had lost my father. I had a daughter so precious to me that I could hardly bear to let her out of my sight. It was then, in the 1980s, that I began to bounce along the bottom of my life. Until then there had been wonderful falls and sickening thrills. I had thought I could control everything. I had gotten enough of what I wanted so that I had the illusion that manipulation was the answer to my problems. With each new start I really believed that my life was going to change. That great original loss—whatever it was— had been the grain of sand around which I built a glistening pearl: my marriage to a substantial man, my writing career, my financial success. I began to hang on for dear life.

I have friends who have lost children. My psychiatrist during those years had lost a daughter. I often dreamed about a little girl lost, and he always said I was dreaming about myself. My friend Ken had lost a son. My friend Sidney lost a daughter. I was drawn to these losses. Last year I went down to Belize to interview Francis Coppola for *Architectural Digest*. Coppola had bought a group of thatch-roofed buildings on a river in the highlands above the jungle and made it into a resort hotel.

I had met Coppola years before when Warren was working for him. I had even had dinner with him in a restaurant and at his house—but of course he didn't remember. It was his birthday, and his daughter, Sofia, and his son Roman and his wife, Ellie, were there in Belize, and he was very much the paterfamilias. I knew that his other son, Gio, had been killed in a boating accident. I knew that they had often come to this place, to Blancaneaux Lodge, as a family when Gio was alive.

I was there to write about architecture, but I wanted to learn about the Coppola family. I wanted to see how a family could survive what I knew they had survived. Francis had also been unfaithful to his wife, I knew; she had written about this in her book about the making of his masterpiece *Apocalypse, Now*. There was a quietness to the way they operated, a loving acceptance of each other and of everything that had happened to them as a family that was nice to be around.

Ellie and I stood out on one of the mahogany porches at twilight and talked. When I mentioned that Warren was in love with another woman, she winced. I had thought I was too tough to care. The next day at a lunch on the porch, Francis turned to me. "You're a good person," he said. I forget what had preceded this announcement, but he said it as if being good was important.

One afternoon I went to the Mayan pyramids. I climbed to the top, where a small, flat platform afforded a view of the scrubby jungle all around me. At the edge of the platform was a three-hundred-foot drop. Down below in the parking lot I could see a group of Americans from the Elderhostel tours eating their lunch. The Mayan kings seemed to be still alive at that height. I felt the presence of those Mayans in the jungle at night. Something about the landscape felt brooding and cruel in spite of the bright orchids springing from the trees and the sound of the river cascading down a rocky waterfall past the lodge.

I used to stop drinking the way I moved to another country, or switched to a new man. I stopped drinking to create a new start for myself. Whenever I stopped drinking, I was filled with the hope that this time, at last, I had the secret. This time, I always thought, was the last time. When I stopped drinking at the suggestion of a sober friend in the fall of 1986, I felt as if my life was coming into focus the way the picture in a camera's viewfinder comes into focus as you turn the lens.

I was trapped in a dead marriage; I just hadn't seen it before. I asked Calvin to move out. I suggested he move to my rent-controlled apartment, which I had been using as an office. That way, Sarah would be able to see him often. He would be in a place she was familiar with. We would share her, but I would be free of the agony of remorse and the guilt of betrayal. It would be the perfect separation, and it worked for a while except for one thing; it broke my Sarah's heart. I would have died for Sarah, but I couldn't keep myself from hurting her. Through my fog of panic and longing, even I saw that.

Once again I was out there alone, flailing around, trying to get—trying to get loved, trying to get famous, trying to get rich, trying to get how to be a good mother. By Eastertime I had decided that the answer was Warren. It was a measure of how at sea I was that a man who was drinking, who lived to drink, could seem an anchor to me. Warren and I came back together with much fanfare. I dropped Bob. Calvin protested loudly, so I presented him with a separation agreement. Warren and I went off to Cuba with his daughters. The morning we were supposed to leave, I saw a small lesion on Sarah's neck. I knew she had been exposed to chicken pox. I left anyway.

We were in Cuba for a week, stuck in the Riviera Hotel on the Malecon while Sarah suffered with terrible chicken pox. I called from Havana every night. I sat on my bed in the Vedado and watched the sun set over the Caribbean and the water turn rosy and purple around the rocks below and listened to her cry. Then Calvin got on the phone. "This stinks," he said. I couldn't leave Cuba and I could hardly stay there. I hated the fading glories, the eager representatives of the state delegated to show us around, the smiles on people's faces. I thought about the Cubans I had known in Tarrytown and their anger at Fidel. One night we went to the Floridita to see the dancers; they bumped and ground, and their feathered hats quivered and their bodies gyrated out of their clothes and I thought I was going to die from the pain of being in my own skin. I needed my daughter; she needed me. In my heart I was reenacting a separation of mother and daughter that resonated from before I could remember. There were days when I told myself that Sarah would be fine, and she was fine. There were days when I told myself that it was good for her father to handle a difficult time with her instead of having the whole thing cushioned by my mothering.

I was right about that, but I remember walking through Old Havana in the tropical heat and feeling as if pain would melt me from the inside. My flesh would begin to droop and then puddle out onto the steaming pavement in front of the Hotel Nacional. I remember having an endless meal at the Bodeguita del Medio and wishing the meal was over. I remember sitting in the air-conditioned cool of the Floridita while Warren drank and counting the hours until I would be at home with my little girl. I remember a party at the Presidential Palace and shaking hands with Fidel and seeing nothing and feeling nothing except that I was in the wrong place. I told everyone that I loved Cuba and that Fidel had worked a miracle there.

That summer, the summer of 1987, Warren decided to run for mayor of San Francisco. I took Sarah to San Francisco to stay at Warren's, but it was hard to find baby-sitters. When Sarah woke up early in the morning, Warren would scoop her up and take her up the hill to a local bar where there was a tank of fish. She liked the fish. She liked Warren's basset hound, Bentley. We rented her favorite videos. Once I left her at a day-care center, and when I went to pick her up, all the children were naked. The little boys and girls were running around playing leapfrog with no clothes on. Sarah had quietly gone into another room with a picture book.

Warren lost and went back to his job at the *San Francisco Examiner*. I never failed to give him a hard time about not being in New York. Every other weekend I got on a plane to San Francisco. When I got there, we would drive; we drove up to Point Reyes and we drove down to Big Sur. In the car, we were friends. Those were our best times, on the way to Gilroy, on the way to Carmel, on the way to Gordo, where an ex-hippie showed us how he hauled huge jade boulders out of the ocean and sliced them into tabletops. When I left, Warren would drive me to the airport and then return the car I had rented. Sometimes he forgot. Once he left the rented car in his drive-way and flew to New York and flew back before he remembered to return it. I laughed about the bill for a thousand dollars bill I got from Hertz Rent a Car. "Warren, I can't afford you," I said. He didn't talk to me for days.

All that time I didn't drink. I went wherever Warren went; I was always in bars. Warren's friend Paddy Nolan, who owned a bar called the Dovre Club, poured me grapefruit juice and tried to sweeten it with vodka. I asked for water. Warren's friend Artie Mitchell made fun of me when we were sitting at any bar where he could catch me. I didn't drink, that was what kept me separate and different. Paddy and Artie are dead now. Warren went right on drinking. Once we were officially back together, Warren thought we should get married and have a child. I told him he was crazy. I said I didn't want to raise two children by myself. I told him to think about it. He said he *had* thought about it, and he still thought it was a good idea. We loved each other, after all. We had always, even back in the sev-enties, talked about having a child. Now we could recover the past. I began to realize that Warren had thought of my marriage to Calvin as nothing more than a downtime in our great love affair.

In the mornings in New York, I took Sarah downstairs to the school bus. She and I—and Warren when he was in New York—lived in the co-op I had bought with Calvin, at the top of an old brick building at the corner of Lexington Avenue and Eighty-first Street. It was a light-filled square of space divided into two front rooms and two bedrooms. My childhood asthma mysteriously returned after a thirty-year remission. I went to an expensive allergist; he prescribed cortisone. At night, Sarah went to sleep at around 7:30. Warren usually stayed up late, and he was usually still in bed in the morning when it was time to get Sarah ready for school. He was often still in bed in the afternoon. When Sarah brought friends home from school, they looked surprised when they glanced into the master bedroom and saw a big man spread out asleep, snoring in the room with the view of other people's terrace gardens.

On the morning of February 6, 1989, I was reading the *Times* in the dining room while Warren slept, and I read a column by Anne Taylor Fleming about the difficulties women had in getting pregnant after the age of forty. Fleming had been unable to get pregnant—she had waited too long—and in her piece she wrote about how few eggs a woman retains after forty, and the desperate, dried-up condition of those eggs; she made it sound almost impossible for an older woman to conceive. I was forty-five, and reading this piece I wondered why I had been bothering to use birth control. I hated the diaphragm; now I could throw it out. I went into the bedroom and woke Warren up.

At the beginning of March, I went to Dr. Buchman. When he asked me if I thought I was pregnant, I laughed.

That morning I was driving to New Haven. I was writing a book about my mother—*Treetops*—and I had found all my grandfather's papers at the Sterling Library at Yale, a research bonanza that I hadn't known about when I started the book. On the Merritt Parkway there was a traffic jam on the Stratford Bridge. We stopped and started, stopped and started. I felt pregnant suddenly. It was as if I wasn't alone, as if someone had just walked into the room. The cars stopped and started, stopped and started. We were moving at about ten miles an hour when the line of cars stopped again. I was thinking about pregnancy and didn't stop in time. My car bumped the car in front of me, and I jammed on the brakes. It wasn't a hard hit, but the man driving the car in front of me opened his door and got out and I saw that he had been holding a cup of coffee as he drove and that when I hit him the coffee splashed all over him, all over his white shirt and his silk tie, all over his jacket and pants; there was even coffee dripping down his face and falling from his eyelashes.

Quad

Warren disappeared on the morning of our wedding, June 10th, 1989. He called from a liquor store on Third Avenue to say he was on his way. He couldn't find the best man. The ushers had trapped him in the bar of the Hotel Edison, making him listen to endless choruses of "Get Me to the Church on Time." As I waited, three hundred invited guests milled around my mother's house in Ossining and filled the tent she had had put up on the lawn under the black walnut tree. They waited for two hours. They drank all the liquor in the house and sent out for more.

By the time we got to the ceremony, even the judge had had too much to drink. My mother had retreated into a familiar quiet rage. The guests had taken over the house; two were in her private bathroom, one was napping on her bed. My seven-year-old Sarah cried throughout the exchanging of the solemn vows. Halfway through, Warren snatched my white broad-

brimmed hat off my head, put it on, and began to dance a little jig. I wonder if, looking on from wherever he was that day,
my father may have had a moment of nostalgia for my First
Love.

On the one hand, I was vowing to love and honor a man
who had brought me great anguish and would soon bring me
tremendous sorrow. On the other hand, I was pregnant with
my beloved son. Also, I was coming to the end of it, I see now.
I was coming to the end of manipulating men and thinking
that other people's pain was funny and believing that if I could
fool you, that was your problem. I was coming to the end of
my drinking. I was coming to the end of being the sassy young
woman I had been, of being the kind of young woman who
could make you laugh at other people even when you were
ashamed of yourself for laughing. I was coming to the end of
that.

For the second time, I married someone because I was pregnant with his child. We got through the wedding, and we got
through the summer, and I hadn't had a drink in three years,
unless you count a few sips here and there or the Communion
wine or sleeping with a man who has just drunk a bottle of
rum. I guess I should say that I hadn't had a drink of my own
in three years.

Then on the night of November 3rd, 1989, I began to have
labor pains. Sarah was with her father for the weekend; he had
just picked her up when the pain started. I was standing in the
living room, debating with Warren what to have for dinner,
when my water broke. At first it was a rush of stained water,

but then, as my contractions began, water poured out of me. Warren lay towels underneath me, and soon there were heaps of wet towels everywhere. Each time a contraction hit, there was water. The contractions got worse. When they began, I started rocking to ease the pain. I practiced the breathing I had learned. The pain, when it came, was unbearable. I called the doctor. He said he would call me in an hour and see how I was doing. I didn't think I could live through another hour of the pain.

There was this stained water everywhere, everywhere, and piles of towels and so much pain, and I was rocking and rocking and when the contractions were coming sooner and sooner and we were thinking about calling the doctor again, Warren went to the fridge and opened a bottle of champagne he had saved. "Here, see if this helps," he said, and he handed me a glass. I drank that glass. It had been three years since I had had a drink. I figured this was a once-in-a-lifetime event. As I drank I promised myself I wouldn't drink after the baby was born. As I drank I felt the pain ebbing out of my body. We killed the bottle, and then the pain went away. My contractions stopped, and I went to sleep. In the morning the doctor's telephone call woke me up. "Where are you," he said. "You should be in the hospital." They gave me an epidural and Pitocin to start the contractions again. Warren disappeared. He came back an hour later wearing sunglasses. I had the baby, my sweet baby boy Quad, coming so naked and perfect into this world. We named him after his father, Warren James Hinckle IV, or Quad for short.

When I got home from the hospital I started drinking again. I decided this whole alcoholism thing had been a huge exaggeration. I was hardly an alcoholic. I didn't have a problem; if anyone had a problem it was Warren. All I drank was a little wine here and there, and then a little more wine here and there. Warren was the alcoholic. I was just drinking white wine. The baby cried and grew and delighted me and delighted his sister. I sold my apartment at the bottom of the market. Warren and I looked for a new place to live. I knew I should buy something, otherwise I would have to pay steep capital gains, but soon enough we were looking at rentals. I don't know how it happened. We looked all over town and then, on the last day we were looking, just before we had almost decided to move to San Francisco—although Warren had lost his job there—we found what seemed to be the answer to our problems. It was a dilapidated gray frame house with a wide, white front porch and a peaked roof, on Ninety-second Street between Park and Lexington Avenues.

The rooms were cramped and shabby, there were only two bedrooms, so the children would have to share a room, but there was an outdoor deck and the place wasn't at all like anything anyone else had. It reflected our loony specialness. It cost much more than we could afford, and that was part of its appeal. We met the landlord, who lived on the first two floors. He was a smart man, a well-read man, who was already quite drunk in the early afternoon. We joined him for sherry, and to toast our new start. We became fast friends. We signed a lease. We felt as if we had come home.

TWENTY-NINE

The Mitchell Brothers

Late one night in the spring of 1991, Warren's friend Jim Mitchell shot and killed his brother Artie. Art and Jim had gotten rich and famous by establishing a pornography empire—they made the movie *Behind the Green Door* and discovered Marilyn Chambers—and their kingdom was the O'Farrell Theater, a strip joint and pornography center on O'Farrell Street in San Francisco that was also an unofficial club of cool for liberal journalists, traveling journalists, writers, and anyone who had enough enthusiasm for the First Amendment and for sex to forgive the Mitchells their repugnant raunchiness and focus on their questionable nobility. The pool room of the O'Farrell Theater was Warren's second home, and I had spent plenty of time there, chatting and drinking the coffee that Warren's friends said was spiked with speed to give the strippers an edge.

I liked taking friends who were visiting San Francisco on the tour of the O'Farrell. We walked through the dressing room, where a dozen strippers were putting makeup on all parts of their bodies; to the balcony above the stage, where they danced for fifteen minutes, then often ended up lap dancing in the audience. Then we visited the cage where men stood in booths and watched women play with each other with an assortment of leather and chain toys, and then there was the Congo Room, where naked women danced in the dark for men seated on banquettes with penis-shaped flashlights. Some of my friends were shocked, others were fascinated. The sexual energy at the O'Farrell made the whole place seem alive. As I looked down from the balcony of New York Live, I could sip a Heineken and spot the yuppie suits of the men who worked in the city and revel in my understanding of American hypocrisy.

Artie Mitchell, the younger brother, had always been the crazy one, and by the time I met him he was scary. I always chalked it up to drugs. I stayed away from him. Jimmy, on the other hand, was charming and reliable. When he said he would do something, he did it. During Warren's mayoral campaign, it was Jimmy who came up with a tow truck for a campaign prank. (Warren towed an abandoned car from a bad neighborhood, where residents had been complaining about it for weeks, to Mayor Diane Feinstein's parking spot at city hall. Sure enough, it was removed in two minutes.) Artie was always the wild one, and Jimmy always cleaned up after him.

Typical of San Francisco in those days was an institution called the Thursday Club. Made up of important town officials, the all-male club met the first Thursday of each month to hear an important speaker. First there was a long cocktail hour, then there was the speech. The speaker—usually an expert in his field, often armed with a carousel of slides—would stand behind the elaborate lectern and start to talk. Within a few minutes someone would urge him to talk louder. Then someone else would yell that the mike wasn't working. Then someone in the back would begin to applaud at every sentence. Then someone else would begin to bark like a dog. The game was to see how long the speaker would go on in the face of what became insuperable and noisy obstacles.

The smart ones got it right away and laughed and joined the party and had another drink. "Have a drink!" an invocation delivered with a slap on the back or an Irish grin was always the password in that world. The less fortunate, or less alcoholic speakers soldiered on, sometimes for ten or fifteen minutes, until the situation got so out of hand that the audience crowded up on the stage, laughing at their own cleverness.

Warren had broken the sacred rule of the Thursday Club—no women. Warren loved to break rules. He had smuggled in two dancers from the O'Farrell Theater—he disguised them in gorilla costumes. But when the Mitchells arrived to speak, dressed in suits and ties, the Thursday Club excited the wild man in Artie, who stood up on the lectern and began to swing the club's expensive new microphone around his head. Typically, Jimmy stayed behind, made the Mitchells' apologies, and paid for the damage. By February 1990, Jimmy was sick of his brother, and when Artie threatened to kill Jim's girlfriend Lisa, something in Jimmy snapped.

Each morning during the trial—the state charged Jim Mitchell with murder—Warren and I left Sarah and Quad with the baby-sitter we had brought to San Francisco. We were writing a book about the Mitchells. A book which would never be published. We drove over to Marin County to the trial, which was in a second-floor courtroom in Frank Lloyd Wright's Marin Civic Center, a building that looks like a UFO that got too heavy for liftoff. Day after day we hung out at the trial, rooting for Jimmy and his defense team, our friends Michael Kennedy and Nancy Clarens. After court we drove up to the house the Kennedys' had rented in San Anselmo and drank martinis.

Jimmy Mitchell got six years; he was released from San Quentin last year. I took pages of notes. Warren and I stopped fighting for a while. We got home to New York in March, but within a few weeks, I knew that I couldn't go on living the way we were living. In the mornings I woke up wanting to die. I was afraid to die. I would tell myself that I would get a cup of coffee first. Then the dogs would have to be walked. Then I would remember my children. Some days I thought it was the house. I was always afraid someone was going to break in. A woman across the street had been raped. Some days I thought it was the city. Most days I blamed it on Warren in general and on his drinking in particular. I decided to do an intervention on him.

In an intervention, an alcoholic's family, colleagues, and friends, supervised by a professional counselor, "surprise" him or her and "lovingly" talk about the effects that the drinker's drinking has had on them and the family and the job. At the end of the intervention, the alcoholic is handed an airplane ticket, and the family urges him to go to a rehabilitation center to get help. If the alcoholic doesn't go, his family will no longer put up with him, his job will no longer be there. This combination of concern and coercion works about half the time—much more often than just asking the alcoholic to get help. I thought that by doing an intervention on Warren I could fix him; I would restore our family to health. This scenario gave me an exhilarating rush.

I went shopping for someone to do an intervention. There were some problems. Warren's daughters didn't want to discuss his alcoholism, and they certainly didn't want to have anything to do with an intervention. Warren's mother didn't want to help either. Warren had already left his job, and his ex-boss was no longer talking to either of us. The normal intervention, when an alcoholic is surrounded by family, colleagues, and friends, seemed impossible. One Friday morning in April, one of the counselors I was interviewing suggested that we would have a better intervention if I stopped drinking. I told her that was no problem. I was not an alcoholic, I patiently explained.

That night, I went to an AA meeting alone. It was a meeting in a basement on Ninety-second Street, just a block away from where I had been living in the gray frame house. It was where my father had gone when he was at Smithers in 1975, and there was a row of people from Smithers sitting at the middle of the group of folding chairs.

One night recently, I rented the movie *The Lost Weekend.* "One of my all-time favorites," the video store manager said. I planned to start watching it once my children were in bed, but my son had trouble falling asleep. He had been staying at his father's apartment down the street, and there is no bedtime at his father's apartment. There are no rules there. As a result when my son comes back to me he can't go to sleep at bedtime, so he lay wide-eyed in his bedroom while I watched the first part of the movie, the part where the movie's hero is hiding his drinking and has a bottle stashed on a string hanging out the window. When his brother is out of the room, he hauls it up and takes a desperate swig.

A few minutes into the movie the doorbell rang. It was Warren, arriving to say good night to our son. Quad was delighted. "Daddy, I was waiting for you," he said. Warren is a big man, and our son's bed creaked as he sat down on it. I could smell vodka and cigarette smoke on his clothes and on his breath. This smell seemed to comfort our son; it is his father's smell.

At midnight, after Quad was asleep and Warren had left, I finished watching the movie. It's a movie about a time when the men all wore hats. Their hair is carefully combed and looks glued into place. They talk as if they are reading from a script, but it's exactly right about alcoholism, and I guess that's what has made it a classic: it's true that an alcoholic will do anything to get a drink. In the movie it's made very obvious that the man is an alcoholic. In life it is often not so obvious. In life there are always ways to fool yourself.

It is the story of a writer with a lovely girlfriend and a loving brother, but the writer keeps ruining everything because he has to drink. He's handsome, and even in the final scenes when he is drinking himself to death, the only indications are a slight day's growth of beard and some gentlemanly sweat. He never loses his hat or forgets to tie his shoes. When he stops drinking he doesn't go through hell or even to an AA meeting—he just stops.

The movie reminded me of how little they knew about alcoholism in those days, those days when everyone was drinking as if drinking was as much a part of life as breathing. They know more now. Everyone knows about Alcoholics Anonymous, for instance. But alcoholism hasn't changed, and the invisible way it works hasn't changed. For most people the definition of alcoholism is still very narrow. Most people still think an alcoholic is someone who is visibly, inescapably out of control. They think an alcoholic is someone who drinks a huge amount of liquor and becomes obstreperous or wild as a result. This narrow definition of alcoholism leaves out more alcoholics than it includes.

Even in my family, where God knows we have experienced enough alcoholism to have drawn a few conclusions and recognize a few signs, alcoholism is still invisible. When I tell my brother that Warren acts the way he acts because he has a disease, my brother tells me to go ahead and believe that if it makes me feel better.

That night I was really glad to hear the door slam behind Warren on his way out. I stood in the doorway of my son's bedroom and watched him sleep in the light from the hall, and I asked God to please bless my little boy.

Stopping Again, Again

Finally, in April of 1991, I found it very, very hard to stop drinking. I needed to pray. I needed to eat hard candy. I needed to make friends who didn't drink. I needed to call them in the middle of the night and cry and rage and complain. In the morning, instead of waking up wanting to die, I stumbled out to the Central Park Reservoir for a run with a friend, one of my new friends, friends who didn't drink. After our run we went to a coffee shop and ate oatmeal. Slowly I began to come to, but waking up meant I was swamped with questions. What about my marriage? How could I ever get out from under the weight of the house filled with our possessions, or the burden of debt to the landlord. Within a few months I moved myself and my children out of the house we couldn't afford—by this time our friend the landlord had initiated a court action—and into an apartment that I could afford. Warren left for San Francisco about a week before the move.

After we moved, I didn't know where Warren was. We had left him and everything of his behind. My little son used to run to the door of the apartment and cry. "I want to go home," he would say. "I want to go home." He was sick the week we moved. His father was gone. I don't know how I lived through that time except that I prayed. I don't know how my children lived through that time either. We were in an apartment where I felt safe, at last, and an apartment that I could afford. I felt as if I had cut the rope that had been dragging me inexorably, incrementally under water. On my son's third birthday I gave a party for four of his friends. I baked a cake and hired a magician. After the party, Quad's father showed up drunk and armed with a huge toy, a car-racing set that was so complicated that it took me an hour to put it together.

Belief in God is autobiographical; it has to come from our experience. I know there is a God because I couldn't stop drinking for very long by myself. I didn't want to be a writer, yet writing is my salvation. I didn't want children, but my children have taught me to love. In spite of everything I could do to mess it up, my life is rich, rewarding, and filled with big joys and small satisfactions. I know there is a God, and in finding that God, I have both the shock of something utterly familiar and the thrill of discovery.

THIRTY-ONE

Healing

I live a quiet life now. Looking backwards, I feel that all those terrible things, those long, sexy afternoons and those betrayals, and further back those griefs and painful sorrows, they all happened to someone else—someone else who just coincidentally happened to be me. In the mornings my daughter goes to school before I'm awake. I hear her in the kitchen making hot chocolate or putting the leash on her dog for a morning walk. Sometimes I get up and keep her company, but these sounds, the sounds of my teenaged daughter getting ready for her day, are the peaceful sounds that begin my morning. I remember other mornings, mornings when I had to put brandy in my coffee just to take the pain away, mornings when I wanted to die.

Then I get up and make my son's lunch. I put a note in the lunch box that tells him I love him. Lately I've stopped being afraid to tell my children that there is a God and that God will take care of them as God has taken care of me. I don't want to make false promises. I walk my boy to school, down the avenue and across the side streets. When the sun is out it shines on his spiky hair and his big smile. So many things make my son smile—the fat buds on the sycamores on our street, a dog that wants to sniff his lunch box, a friend passing us as we get near school.

When I turned fifty, something changed in me. Before that I had been searching, searching, searching. They say that drinking is a low-level search for God. Those ecstatic rushes of feeling *did* seem to bring me closer to the center of the world. I was desperate to connect with something, anything that would give me a moment of peace. Nothing worked. Now I have whole minutes of peace. Sometimes I have entire days of peace.

I used to go to church with my father on Sunday. I went because it was a time to be alone with him. I went because after church he was always in a good mood, and sometimes we went out for breakfast together. I didn't like the dampness of the pews or the gloom of the chancel or the feeling that I was being watched by other members of the congregation—and by God—and somehow found wanting. Church made me profoundly self-conscious. We always went to the eight o'clock Communion service. We went to All Saints at the corner of Scarborough Road in Scarborough, where we heard the Reverend Bill Arnold drone through the service. In Rome we went to St. Paul's Within the Walls, the American Church, where I was baptized and confirmed in the spring. In Ossining we went to Trinity Church, where my father made fun of the minister's weird West Indian accent. Often, after the Gospel was read but before the Nicene Creed, I would get the sniffles. I was sometimes already wheezing. My nose would sponta- neously begin to run and itch. I never had Kleenex. I would try and snort the problem away, but that just made it worse. My father never brought Kleenex either. The entire second half of the service, until we went up to the rail to take Communion, would be spent trying to control my embarrassing condition.

My children ask me if I believe that we will meet my father when we are dead. They are afraid of death; they are afraid that I will die and leave them alone. My daughter fears for her own father, who is in his seventies now and has been sick. I am also afraid for them because I know how fragile we all are, how fragile it all is.

In another way I am not afraid, because whatever happens is God's will. At night I lie in the arms of the man I love with my children asleep in the next room. "Are you ready?" he says. "Are you ready for sleep?" I imagine that we are old, still lying in each other's arms. I imagine that my children are grown and have taken up their own lives. I imagine that he is asking if I am ready to go gently into that good night. "Yes," I say. "Yes, I am ready."

THIRTY-TWO

The Places I Went

When I was about ten I came home from school one day convinced that my father had to drive me to Fort Ticonderoga. We had been studying Ethan Allen and his Green Mountain Boys and the way they silently, one night, took over the fort while the British were sleeping. The fort was still there on a bluff above the Hudson, and I had to see it. As a child I was sometimes seized by these obsessions—the first one, when I was six, was that I had to have a baby grand piano. It was my mother who was impressed by these obsessions. She went to an auction house and got me a piano. I never played it. She made me take lessons. They were torture. I didn't really want the piano, of course, and she couldn't give me what I really wanted.

So it was my mother who drove me to see Fort Ticonderoga. She drove and I chattered. After lunch my job was to pass her glasses of milk spiked with scotch. Everyone drank when they drove in those days. Driving was tedious; drinking relieved the tedium. My father always had a bottle when he drove. So when I grew up I thought it was moderate of me to just drink beer when I was driving. Driving was drinking. I drove across the country to California and back, to Colorado and back. It wouldn't have occurred to me not to drink.

I went to Paris with Warren on my fiftieth birthday. Neither of us was drinking. The intervention I had tried to plan never happened. Instead, after we moved, Warren had stopped drinking. He had moved in with us in the new apartment on East End Avenue—of course half the time he was in California, but we were a family again. In Paris we went to a restaurant that had a boat beached on the sidewalk in front of it. We went to a restaurant where they soft-boiled an egg, took out the egg, mixed it with truffles and foie gras, and siphoned it back into the shell. Being with Warren when he wasn't drinking was like living under a storm cloud. I always had the feeling something terrible was about to happen. The air around him was all turbulence and anger. He tried; I tried. It didn't work.

By the end of the summer, Warren was drinking again, but I didn't know it. I suspected it. I thought about following him, but the image of me peering into the windows of the neighborhood bars looking for my husband was too much for me to bear. It wasn't until October, when he walked into the apartment red faced and drunk, that I knew for sure. I remember the moment. A friend was there, and my children, and we all gawked. It was the end of the dream that we could be a family—right there, over in a moment, with Warren being very jolly and smelling like gin. After that he promised to go to a rehab, but he never went. After that it just got worse and worse, and the whole thing was dying but none of us could admit it. My daughter started throwing up everything she ate. I cried all the time. Warren and I went to couples therapy. He started missing appointments. He rented an office down the street. My lawyer told me I would have to change the locks on my apartment. I didn't think I could live with Warren another minute. He was drinking more and more. I thought if I didn't live with Warren it would ruin my little boy's life. He loves his father.

One night, Warren said he was going up to Elaine's. I said well fine, but if you come in late don't wake me up. He said very well, he would sleep at his office. That was the end of it. I never shared air with him again. Slowly I began to be able to breathe. The storm moved on, the turbulence settled down. Now my heart is still. But my little boy still loves a man who can't be depended on, whose love is an alternating current of passion, who has to let you down just at the moment you need him the most.

I grew up with a secret. My family did have a skeleton in the closet. Nothing was as it seemed. In his journals, as early as the early 1960s, my father is in agony over his desire for men and his affairs with men. This private agony took a tremendous amount of his moral and emotional energy. My father was often distracted, and no wonder. His focus was on saving his marriage—a marriage continually threatened by his hidden sexual life. To hide the reality, he created a potent myth, the myth of the shabby country squire—the myth of the family whose beauty and talents would win them entrée into the society from which they had been banned. We had the lost Eden, the world of the Boston Brahmins, we had our own glorious past—and we had our marching orders. We grew up in a weird kind of incubator in which the parts we were assigned to play were much more important than anything else.

But the real family secret was not my father's bisexuality, it was the drinking. My father's fear of exposure, his terrified reaction to others' exposure—in those years other men were discredited for things he did—his intense, life-or-death desire to appear to be something he wasn't: that was nothing. That was a secret that could be discovered in an instant. It *was* discovered in an instant. I read my father's journals and I knew and that was that. The drinking was a different kind of secret and a more dangerous one. It wasn't hidden, it was completely visible. Because it was completely visible, the drinking was a secret that we kept from ourselves.

There was no private agony about hiding the fact that we drank or even that my father drank. What alcohol does is hidden until the very end, and even when it's exposed it hides. I don't think my father ever knew—even after seven years of being sober and going to AA meetings and courting rigorous honesty—I don't think he ever knew how much drinking had distorted our family life. I am just now beginning to know.

The recovery people say that alcoholism is like an elephant in the living room, and that living with alcoholism induces insanity because everyone has to pretend that the elephant isn't there. Pretending that things are not as they seem—that you don't see what you do see, that you don't hear what you do hear—makes children crazy. We had the elephant of alcoholism, but it was completely invisible. The way we drank was entirely normal, and the proof of that was that everyone we knew drank that way. It never dawned on me, or any of us, that the people my family knew were chosen *because* they drank that way—anymore than I realized that in choosing Warren I disguised my own alcoholism.

Even these days, when everyone thinks they know about alcoholism, it still hides. No one imagines that their own drinking is a problem. No one guesses that young people, people whose faces aren't red, whose bodies aren't bloated, who don't stumble and slur, might still be completely controlled by their drinking. Alcohol warps the mind long before it even begins on the body—that's why we love it so. Alcoholism is still invisible, even now.

Even when my father took me to AA meetings I never dreamed I might be an alcoholic. If you had told me that the problems in my life came from my breathing, it would have made as much sense to me as if you said the problems in my life came from my drinking. Alcohol was already controlling me in its powerful, cunning ways. When there were things I didn't want to face, I took a drink. It worked. If it was the feelings of a woman whose husband I was sleeping with, or his children, or if it was the problem of what to wear to a party, or if it was the politics of *Newsweek* magazine, the cure was the same. I had a glass or two of wine, or a scotch; that was what everyone did. The next morning the things I didn't want to face didn't loom so large. I thought that was part of being a grown-up, and in the world where I was a child, I wasn't wrong.

And somehow, I spent all those years searching, searching for someplace where I did belong, and I finally found it by making my own family, and I couldn't even do that right, but I finally found it anyway. I accept what happened to me as just what happened. My family was aberrant, but aberrant from what? We were who we were, just as my children and I are who we are. Last night I dreamt that I lost my son. I looked around and he wasn't there. This is my worst fear, but even my worst fears are not so bad anymore. I have a kind of jerry-built faith that I've been able to cobble together a little bit at a time. My faith has a Rube Goldberg aspect to it—there are plenty of places where I lift a weight and a marble goes down a chute and hits a lever that activates a cog wheel, which turns a crank.

It seems as though my belief in God should take up more space in this book, but it is intensely private and truly beyond my ability to describe. I don't understand God; I just believe in God. I have faith that there is a benevolent force at large in the universe, and my life has reflected that faith. I have experienced God's grace in abundance, and I am grateful for that. Most of all, though, I don't hope to persuade anyone else to believe in God. Although magazine and newspaper polls show that most Americans believe in God and that most of us pray regularly, this is not true in my community here in New York City. Many people I know think that they are too smart for God, and they are very smart. God is for people who are uneducated, they think, or not too smart, or weak and needy. Maybe they're right. It's not something I argue about; if I did I'd be happy to lose.

Faith in God is hard to maintain these days, but I do feel that it's taken me fifty years to discover what centuries of civilized people already knew, and that we, in our time, somehow forgot. I wouldn't be able to believe in a God I could describe in mere words. I do believe, though, that the answer to life's questions is a faith in something outside of life; belief in God.

My last drink was a glass of white wine, poured and sipped in the floor-through living and dining room of the frame house on Ninety-second Street. Warren was on the telephone. The children were asleep downstairs—Q in his crib, Sarah in the bunk bed. After they slept, I went upstairs, curled up with a book or a magazine, and tried to stay awake until Warren was ready for bed. I couldn't. Instead I drank the white wine, and read until my eyelids drooped, and I went downstairs to bed alone. I didn't even know what the trouble was.

I didn't know I had to stop drinking, and I didn't know I could stop drinking. I didn't know that I had to leave Warren, and I didn't know that I could leave Warren.

At night now, when my children Quad and Sarah have gone to bed and I have read for a while, I walk down the hall to turn out the kitchen lights. The dog is curled up on a chair in the living room, and I shoo her off. On the way back to bed, I look into my children's rooms. My daughter is nestled under the covers; my son has thrown off his quilt and is already sprawled across the bed. I take a sweet, deep breath. I watch my children sleeping safely and rejoice.

Acknowledgments

I am extremely grateful to the following people for their help.

Chuck Adams, Renata Adler, James Atlas, Richard Avedon, and Miriam Arond. My esteemed Bennington colleagues: Sven Birkerts, Alice Mattison, Jill McCorkle, Jason Shinder, Amy Hempel, Donald Hall, Robert Bly, Lynn Freed, Bob Schacocchis, Marie Howe, Doug Bauer, Askold Melnyczuk, Tom Ellis, Maria Flook, Kate Daniels, Lucy Grealey, April Bernard, Susan Dodd, David Lehman, Betsy Cox, Tree Swenson, George Packer, Chuck Bock, Jamie Clarke, and the incomparable Liam Rector.

Larry Bergreen, Carl Bernstein, Bill Wilson, Patty Bosworth, Carol Bowie, Ken Burrows, Catherine Callaghan, Jane Carr, Andrew Cheever, Fred Cheever, John M. Cheever, John Cheever, Mary Cheever, Janet Maslin Cheever, Ben Cheever, Cher, Marcelle Clements, Judy Collins, Colleen Croft, Gypsy da Silva, Andrew Jakabovics, Elif Batuman, Peter Davis, Dr. Colleen Edwards, Dr. Ted Jacobs, Dr. Ramon Murphy, Dr. Andrea Marks, Dr. Sharon Diamond, and Dr. Chris Beels. Ron

Galen, Lenny Golay, Mary Gordon, Hannah Griswold, Frank Griswold, Phoebe Griswold, Eliza Griswold, Pete Hamill, Whitney Hansen, Robert Haserot, Rebecca Head, Quad Hinckle, Warren James Hinckle III, Jane Hirschfield, Jane Hitchcock, Priscilla Hodgkins, Mary Beth Hughes, John Irving, Erica Jong, Elaine Kaufman, Michael and Eleanore Kennedy, Cheryl King, and the fabulous Michael Korda.

Ken Lauber, Fran Lebowitz, Muriel Lloyd, Arthur Loeb, Bridget Love, Malachi McCourt, Jim Mitchell, Artie Mitchell, Rick Moody, Adam Moss, Paddy Nolan, Leigh Norell, Ned O'Gorman, Paige Petersen, Mark Piel, Eric Rayman, Paige Rense, Michael Rice, Kathy Rich, Gail Richards, Ruthie Rogers, Richard Rogers, Roo Rogers, Bo Rogers, Kitty Ross, Ginger Rothe, Maggie Scarf, Linda Sexton, Ed Specht, Eugene and Clare Thaw, Judith Thurman, Sarah Liley Cheever Tomkins, Calvin Tomkins, John Updike, Jeanette Watson, Cheryl Weinstein, Jackie Weld, David Whitney, Andrew Wylie, Reba White Williams, Margot Willkie, and Michael Wollaeger. My Winternitz cousins—Helen, Bob, both Johns, Sally, Bill, and Tom.

Also, Ofelia Zapata, Sidney Zion, the community of the Convent of the Sacred Heart, the inspirational Shelley Harwayne, and the teachers and parents of the Manhattan New School.

Thank you!

New York City, July 1998